THE

good

GOODBYE

How to Navigate Change and Loss in Life, Love, and Work

GLADYS ATO, PSY.D.

The Good Goodbye: How to Navigate Change and Loss in Life, Love, and Work
Copyright © 2017 by Gladys Ato, Psy.D.

ISBN: 978-0-9994691-0-1

Published by Bridging Consciousness Publishing 2017
San Francisco, CA, United States

www.bridging-consciousness.com

Cover design and book art design © 2017 by Stef Etow

The content of this book is for educational purposes only. It is not intended to be a substitute for evaluation or treatment by a licensed professional. The information contained in this book should not be used to diagnose or treat a mental health issue without consulting a qualified provider. The use of this book does not convey any doctor-patient relationship.

Table of Contents

HOW TO USE
THIS BOOK

I wrote this book for anyone who wants to rise above the challenges of saying goodbye and learn to successfully adapt to change—whether it's a career change, a relationship breakup or divorce, the death of a loved one, or a change in your beliefs.

The ability to successfully adapt to change is the one trait that separates those who master life's challenges from those who become crippled by them. Even if goodbyes trigger an internal panic button that makes you grip on tighter to what you don't want to lose, you can get through them with greater self-confidence and trust. And it starts with a simple reframing of what change and goodbyes mean so you can make room for the good that comes with them.

Use this book as a starting place to understand where you've struggled with change and how you'd like to deal with it in the future. Read the book from start to finish—if you jump around, you'll miss important information in Part 1 that helps lay the foundation for Parts 2 and 3. Take breaks to write down your reactions, and stay mindful of your thoughts as you reflect on how the book relates to your own experiences.

To help you get the most of out this book, I created two free bonuses for you: The Good Goodbye Blueprint, a supplemental workbook to apply The Good Goodbye® approach, and The Good Goodbye members-only site (more details below).

All you need to do to get immediate access to your free bonuses is go to the website below:

https://drgladysato.com/the_good_goodbye_bonuses/

The Good Goodbye Blueprint is a free workbook containing practical, psychology-based exercises that show you how to apply The Good Goodbye approach to a change or loss you're currently struggling with. I recommend that you download your free workbook now and use it as a place to take notes while reading the book. Then, when you're done reading the book, complete the workbook exercises.

Your second free bonus, The Good Goodbye members-only site, was created to address one of the biggest pitfalls of personal growth books: being left on your own to implement what you've learned.

How often do you feel a "I can do this!" high after reading a book, only to find that it lasts for about 1-2 weeks? What happens? A work deadline creeps up. Family obligations pull away your attention. The daily grind takes over and that 'high' is quickly replaced with a sense of letdown.

I want to make sure you have ongoing support in applying The Good Goodbye approach so you see results. Here are a few things you can look forward to receiving in this site:

- Access to a community of change-makers who are transforming their struggle with goodbyes into inspired action to help themselves and others adapt to change with more ease.

- Curated resources and strategies that help you further apply The Good Goodbye approach to your life.

- Live video sessions where I'll be sharing how The Good Goodbye approach is applied to everyday situations.

- Guest appearances by personal empowerment experts.

When you go to the website to claim your free workbook, you'll also receive an email with instructions to immediately access the members-only site.

These bonuses are yours for free as a thank you for purchasing this book. I know firsthand how isolating it can be to go through a big change or loss and how hard it often is to then ask for support. I want to help you transform your old ways of dealing with goodbyes into an approach that allows you to thrive and confidently adapt to any change that life throws your way, while being part of a supportive community that cheers you on through it all.

Visit the link below to get your free access:

https://drgladysato.com/the_good_goodbye_bonuses/

Lastly, please use this book for educational purposes only. It is not to be used to diagnose or treat a mental health issue. While the book is informed by my training and expertise as a clinical psychologist and former psychotherapist, it is not intended to be a substitute for evaluation or treatment by a licensed professional.

I can't wait to get started with you!

Con gratitud,

Dr. Gladys Ato

INTRODUCTION

This book is a compilation of my 20 years of clinical experience as a psychotherapist, mental health consultant, and higher education executive leader, and 15 years of a dedicated self-healing journey involving traditional therapy and sacred healing practices. The perspectives I offer are based on research, direct intervention, and observation on the ways we cope with change and loss. My hope is that this book will provide you guidance, relief, and inspiration to develop new ways to deal with change so you can go through it with more ease.

Having personally struggled with change and loss for several years, I saw the ways my life was being negatively impacted. My fear of facing what scared me about goodbyes kept me stuck. Yet in 2003, I developed a new outlook on goodbyes that changed my life forever. I applied this outlook in my life and shared it with friends, clients, and colleagues to help them create a "good goodbye."

Although I was informally helping people implement my philosophy of a good goodbye, I didn't yet understand that it could be a larger concept with greater impact. However, this changed in 2013, when I was faced with a large organizational transition.

Shortly after becoming president of The National Hispanic University (NHU), the first 4-year accredited university in the United States devoted to Latinos, I learned the institution was facing grave challenges. These challenges ultimately led the board of directors to decide to close the university after 34 years of existence. As the president, I was responsible for shepherding the university community through the closure. I had never shut down an organization—I certainly didn't learn how to do that in graduate school. But what I did know was loss and grieving, and leading teams through change. And I now knew what it meant to find the good in goodbye.

Over the course of one and a half years, I worked tirelessly with devoted members of the university community to bring all operations to a close. I shared my philosophy of a good goodbye, and the term caught on. Through every strategic plan we created, this philosophy was at the forefront. The success we had at turning a painful ending into a transformational, healing experience is one that I hope every person and community can be a part of. My experience at NHU gave me the courage to build upon my philosophy of a good goodbye and develop The Good Goodbye® approach so I could share it with others on a larger scale.

The approach comprises of psychology and science-based strategies that help you strengthen your emotional adaptability and resilience to the stress of change. It is a straightforward framework for redefining goodbyes so you can learn to embrace change, cope more effectively with loss, and close the chapter on any unfinished endings that are keeping you stuck in the past.

This book is not an overnight fix to your struggles; there is no quick way to heal the pain of losing what has changed. Finding the courage to get to a new place in life where you are able to adapt to change with more ease will require your full investment. No one can do the work for you or give you all the answers you're seeking. But The Good Goodbye approach will help you shift your perception about what is possible for you, which will make your work less complicated.

Each time you use The Good Goodbye approach to face a new change or work through a past loss that rocked your world, it will become even more intuitive and help-ful to you. If you're going through a very recent change or loss and the approach doesn't make sense for you right now, I recommend you read Chapters IV, V, VI and complete the self-care exercises in The Good Goodbye Blueprint to understand how to manage your fresh shock and grief and get to a place where you can breathe again. At that point, you can revisit the approach to sup-port your ongoing process of healing.

Dealing with change and loss is a complex issue, so please be mindful of what your needs are as you cope. If you're having an especially difficult time moving through a loss, your emotional or physical health is suffering, or you feel hopeless or stuck, enroll the support of a li-censed professional counselor, therapist, or healer. They are here to help ease your pain. Don't make things any harder than they need to be— allow yourself to be open to receiving their support.

On the pages that follow, you'll read the stories of people going through major life changes. Their stories portray the challenges we commonly face when saying goodbye, whether it be to a loved one, career, major organizational or societal change, or long-held belief. Their experiences are not unique—you likely will see yourself in one or more of the stories. The stories are unaltered, and each person has been given a pseudonym to protect his or her identity. As you read their stories, take time to reflect on how their experiences relate to your own. Write down your reflections and refer to them as you complete *The Good Goodbye Blueprint* exercises.

As part of my research for this book, I administered a survey to a large group of adults between the ages of 27-75 to test my hypothesis that the collective story we have about change and goodbyes is negative, which keeps us from acceptance and closure. When the survey participants were asked to name three words to describe the feelings they associate with goodbyes, the top three responses, in order of frequency, were:

Sadness
Anxiety
Anger

If you have a negative view of what goodbyes mean, you're going to interpret future change though this negative lens, rather than allow yourself to create a new experience. To help you work through these tough emotions and develop a new definition of goodbyes, I'll provide a framework for understanding The Good Goodbye approach in the first part of the book.

I'll explain why goodbyes are hard to deal with by introducing you to attachment theory, a psychological model that explains the dynamics of human relationships. You'll learn how early childhood experiences form a template from which you determine how to feel, think, and act as an adult when facing change.

I'll address how to adapt to and manage the stressful emotions and physiological responses that are a natural reaction to coping with a change. You'll understand how over-relying on common defense mechanisms such as avoidance or denial can backfire and keep you from moving forward.

We'll also dive into the role of loss and grieving, two major components associated with any change. You'll identify what happens to your mind, body, and heart when you face a change so you can be better informed on how best to take care of your needs.

Once you have a solid understanding of why goodbyes are hard to begin with, we'll dive into the second part of the book, in which I outline the five pillars of The Good

Goodbye approach: Acceptance, Understanding, Gratitude, Forgiveness, and Saying Goodbye. These pillars reflect the desired outcomes survey respondents identified, as well as insights gleaned from my professional and personal experience, research and observation of what people want when going through change and loss. I will provide you insights and tools designed to shift your narrative around goodbyes and help you become more emotionally adaptable to change. You'll develop a clear understanding of how to use this practical framework for navigating future change with more ease.

In the last part, I'll present different scenarios for putting The Good Goodbye approach into practice, with the aim of helping you apply it to a situation that you're preparing to let go. Make sure to complete the exercises in your free workbook, *The Good Goodbye Blueprint*, to further learn how to apply the approach. As I shared earlier, my recommendation is that you download the workbook now, use it as a place to take notes as you read the book, then complete the workbook exercises in their entirety once you finish reading the book.

The more change and loss you go through, the more opportunities you'll have to look at what goodbyes mean to you. Use this book and *The Good Goodbye Blueprint* as guides to keep you focused on what you most desire to get out of each of those moments.

I know firsthand the suffering that comes with staying stuck, not accepting what's changed, and not making room for something new in the future. That suffering keeps you from creating a life you love. It doesn't have to be that way. I'm honored to support you in rewriting your story around goodbyes so you can experience positive change with more ease. Let's dive in.

I.

THE POWER
OF GOODBYE

"

Before a new chapter is begun, the old one has to be finished: Tell yourself that what has passed will never come back...Close some doors. Not because of pride, incapacity or arrogance, but simply because they no longer lead somewhere.

– Paulo Coelho

Chapter 1

Presence Takes Practice

"Like an ability or muscle, hearing your inner
wisdom is strengthened by doing it."

-Robbie Gass

I was working as a psychotherapist at an outpatient clinic in the Bay Area when I received a call from my father. "Your mother had a stroke, mi hija." After nearly 30 years of marriage and raising two daughters to adulthood, my mom spent her last hour of life in a therapy session recounting her 54 years of existence. It was the first time she had sought help for her depression which had plagued her since childhood. Halfway through the session, she was seized by the agonizing pain of a brain aneurysm. In transit to the hospital, she died.

Nothing can prepare you for the loss of a loved one. My world turned upside down that day and every belief and construct I had relied on to define how my world worked were all of a sudden meaningless. The tragedy of my mom's sudden death filled my very large Latino family with profound grief and pain. She was the pillar of the family and now that the pillar was gone, would the family structure crash to the ground?

Fingers were pointed, blame was cast, anger was expressed. I blamed myself for being selfish in wanting material things for which my mom worked nonstop to provide. I projected my anger at others to avoid feeling that I should have prevented her death by helping her seek therapy earlier. I was a psychologist, for goodness' sake. Shouldn't I have seen the depths of her depression and known the ways her lack of sleep and poor self-care could affect her blood pressure and overall health? Should I have left her on life support at the hospital, even though the doctor had pronounced her brain dead, in the hopes that a miracle would occur? Did I lack faith and pull the plug too soon?

These and other seedlings of guilt, remorse, shame, and self-blame immediately started to sprout. And had it not been for the miracle I experienced, those seeds would have easily grown into sturdy trunks of self-hatred and self-blame, leading my heart to shut down as each passing day of my life continued without my mom.

On the day of her funeral, we arrived at the cemetery. My heart was so heavy with grief that I found that simply walking and breathing required every ounce of energy in my body. My vision was foggy with unending tears. I knew I was next to my father and sister, but aside from that, I had no ability to give my attention to what was happening around me.

Suddenly, the music of a mariachi band swirled in my ears. My senses awakened, and I realized the oddity of having such beautiful, celebratory music playing at a funeral. Was this appropriate? Who hired the band? I believed moments of loss were dark and heavy. The lightness of the music contradicted this belief, challenging me to let in the joy. But the grief of having lost my mom masked the light.

As the mariachi continued playing and my mom's coffin was carried to her final resting place, my confusion was diminished by a profound explosion in my heart. All of a sudden, I felt infused with copious amounts of the purest love and joy I had ever experienced. I was feeling my mom's divine essence, and it did not consist of pain, regret or suffering. I sensed her acceptance of having left this earth and the exhilarating exuberance she felt in her new state of being.

All of a sudden, I heard myself blurting out to my father, "Mommy is SOOOO HAPPY right now!!" My dad muttered, "Yeah." His stifled response—acknowledgment mixed with disbelief that I was speaking this way at the funeral—yanked me back to the reality of everyone around me crying and mourning my mom's loss. Yet I couldn't deny what I was feeling throughout my entire being.

My mom suffused me with the knowing that she was at peace with her death and that her spirit would never abandon me. She gave me the greatest gift I've ever received in my life: acceptance. In that moment, I accepted her death. I accepted that her leaving this earth was the best thing for her and our family. I accepted that I had lost my mother. In acceptance, I found the strength that would carry me forward as I understood I would never be able to feel her embrace again. In that profound moment, as my heart filled with celebration and joy, joining with the existing grief and sorrow, I learned what it meant to embody a Good Goodbye.

Through my mom's grace, I learned that we have the capacity to hold both grief and joy at the same time, which allows us to experience loss wholeheartedly. When we embrace this paradox and invite in the duality of emotions, we open ourselves to experiencing the healing power of goodbye.

With every transition, change, and loss, the gifts of healing and closure await you.

It can be so easy to cut yourself off from the experience when you feel overwhelmed by loss (or the threat of loss). But if you allow yourself to be present to face the transition, feel the loss, and see and receive the gifts, the impact is life-changing.

In a society that embraces racing through each day on autopilot to keep up with constant stress, we're not accustomed to being present. To keep up with the fast pace of life, we train our minds to be "forward thinking"—and as a result, thinking about "right here, right now" is much harder.

Think about a time when you focused on being present. Maybe you took a yoga class, tried a meditation practice, or went on a hike in nature. Chances are that at first, your mind struggled to let go of all the thoughts of what you had to do later that day, and what you forgot to do yesterday. Being still and present was as easy as getting a puppy to stay.

This is because presence takes practice. It requires you to be connected to what you're feeling, thinking, and doing in the here and now; to let go of trying to figure out what's going to happen in the future; and to release your grip on ruminating on the past. When you are present, you face yourself, others, and the situation 100%. I'll give you an example.

Several years ago, when I was a university professor, a student came to my office in tears. She told me she couldn't complete a class presentation because she was overwhelmed with all her personal responsibilities. I asked her if there was anything about the assignment that was scaring her; she reiterated that she just had too many other things on her plate.

In my 30+ years of public speaking experience, I've seen all kinds of creative ways people try to get out of speaking, so I took a different tack. I shared with the student that I used to try getting out of my class presentations when I was in school. She then confessed that she was terrified of public speaking. By putting so much energy into trying to distract me with an excuse, she avoided being present with what was really happening: she was afraid and needed help. Once we acknowledged that truth, we could address the fear that was showing up in the present moment. I could now be a source of support to her rather than reinforce her avoidance.

While it might feel easier to run in the other direction, if you can sustain the present experience (no matter how difficult or uncomfortable it is), you'll find it brings a deeper connection to, and deeper understanding of, what you're going through. It will also help you make better decisions that honor all that you're dealing with. The same concept applies to moments of change and the narrative you've created about what goodbyes mean. What do I mean by "narrative"? Well, your life is a series of experiences. For each experience, you create a narrative, a story, telling yourself what happened to help you make sense of what occurred. Your perception of who you are, what others mean to you, and how things work in the world are reflected in each story you create.[1] Your mind uses these stories as templates for how you interpret future situations.

If you can be present with what's showing up when facing a change or loss, let go of past stories of suffering, and avoid filling up the future with assumptions of pain, you arrive to the magic of the present moment where anything is possible. From that point, you can decide what story you'll create to define that moment moving forward.

I know this is difficult. As we've discussed, many of us create stories to reinforce the belief that goodbyes are painful and must be avoided. But oftentimes, the discomfort of keeping up such a story becomes painful and exhausting in its own right.

As a psychotherapist, I have frequently treated the complications of people struggling to deal with changes such as divorce, job loss, change in family dynamics, loss of a loved one, or moving to a new home. My clients feared facing a future where things were different from what they had planned, and that fear grew as they tried avoiding dealing with things. Over time, depression, anxiety, somatic pain, or complicated grieving arose. When things were unbearable enough, they finally sought help. As a trained professional, I provided them with tools they could use to ride the waves of change more effectively.

These tools helped them transform the stories they had about goodbyes. They became increasingly adaptable to change, capable of being more present with their experience, and were able to understand it with a new perspective. This expanded understanding helped increase their emotional resilience and led to more ease in successfully adapting to change in the future.

In this book, I'll provide you the same tools so you can benefit from them as you go through your own changes. First, it's important to understand why times of change are so difficult and how the way you cope today as an adult is connected to your early experiences with goodbyes growing up.

Chapter II

The Role of Attachment and Self-Soothing in Times of Change

"Though surely to avoid attachments for fear of loss is to avoid life."

–Lionel Shriver

You know saying goodbye provokes difficult feelings like sadness, anxiety, and anger. Regardless of whether life was easy or hard growing up, or how well-adjusted you are as an adult, dealing with goodbyes and the associated feelings can still be tough. So why is it such a struggle to say goodbye and get to a place of closure?

The answer is simple: you attach yourself to people and things—to loved ones, objects, the perceived stability of a job, and your beliefs about how things work in the world. In the field of developmental psychology, attachment is defined as "a deep and enduring emotional bond that connects one person to another across time and space."[2] As a human, you have an instinctual drive to at-tach—it helps you feel protected, secure, and loved. This instinct is with you from the moment you are in your mother's womb—this is the first attachment you form.

As you grow up, you also form attachments with other significant figures in your life such as another parent, teachers, neighbors, or relatives. These early attach-ments shape your response to goodbyes, as you observe how those around you cope with and talk about change and loss. They give you a template for how to deal with things, which, over time, contributes to your coping style and how easily you bounce back from life's challenges.[3] To understand why you respond to goodbyes and change in your own unique way, it's valuable to look back at your early experiences.

When you are faced with the loss of a person or some-thing you value, your attachment to that person or thing must change as well. This triggers a natural stress re-sponse, a physiological and emotional reaction that is your body's way of responding to the change in attach-ment. The stress response may manifest in a variety of ways: a racing heart, shallow breathing, a loss or gain of appetite, or a feeling of panic. Obviously, stress doesn't just show up in response to major life events. It's a nat-ural part of human functioning and arises when you face emotional tension or pressure or feel overwhelmed in response to any demand for change.[4]

Childhood causes a lot of stressors—stress in response to hunger, a wet diaper, and temporary separation from your parent are just a few examples. And this is where the "template" I mentioned above is formed. If your early attachment figures (parents, caregivers, etc.) consistently responded to you by providing security, comfort, and a sense of protection when you were stressed, you record those experiences in your memory. These attachment figures become templates of "secure attachment" that help you learn to get through the stress and return to a state of calm, which is referred to as homeostasis.[5]

With repetition and time, you are more likely to internalize what it feels like to be soothed in times of stress. As you grow older, you use this template of secure attachment to develop your coping style and provide yourself with the sense of security and comfort you experienced early on. This is known as emotional self-regulation or self-soothing.[6]

Being able to regulate your response to stress benefits you greatly as you go through life. Yet, even if you do well managing stress, dealing with change can still be hard—after all, change means losing an attachment to someone or something you value. You still need to go through the process of adjusting to the loss. But having the tools to effectively regulate your emotions helps you work through the stress of losing an attachment with more ease.

When you don't have the childhood experiences of being comforted in times of stress, it can be harder to effectively cope as an adult. Child development research has demonstrated that children who go without such comfort from a secure attachment have a hard time learning how to cope with stress later in life. They adapt by relying on whatever coping tools they do have, which can manifest into anxiety or mood disorders, difficulty expressing their needs or being in touch with their emotions, or engaging in self-destructive behaviors such as substance abuse or acting out through aggression toward others.[7, 8] Not knowing how to deal with stress in an adaptive manner becomes an isolating, unhealthy experience. Being unable to regulate their emotions to return to homeostasis leaves them distrusting of their own capacity to effectively cope with a stressful event. Rather than develop that instinctual drive to connect and attach to others to get through tough times, they learn people aren't there for them when they're scared, and so the best response is to disconnect or detach.

As your life unfolds, your coping style and template of attachment established in childhood will continue to be shaped by the myriad of experiences you go through and the other attachments you form. You may find that you have a hard time dealing with change and goodbyes as an adult whereas as a child, you didn't struggle as much. Or, you may have struggled establishing secure attachments as a child that made it hard to deal with the stress of change, but later on, learned healthy ways to cope. In either case, it's important to realize that it's not a matter of something being wrong with you, or falling back on blaming your childhood if you have a hard time with goodbyes. Rather, it's about being present with your experience, looking at what's happened in your life to shape your adult responses, and adjusting what you need to cope in a healthier way.

If you know you struggle to cope and self-soothe in times of stress, it's important to understand how this is complicating your response to the stress of saying goodbye. This is where presence with your experience is important. You may find ways to deny or rationalize your experience so it doesn't seem like a big deal, but inside you're hurting. This denial makes it harder to find better ways to manage change and not get stuck.

Be present with your natural need for security and comfort. Pay attention to how you struggle. Think about how you were shown to cope early on, and determine what you need moving forward to develop greater resilience. Doing this will help you avoid spiraling into low self-worth, depression, anxiety, or other significant psychological difficulties.[9]

The goal in developing a healthy coping style is to learn to feel the stress associated with change and goodbyes and develop a resilience that gets you through the thick of it without abandoning your needs.

In addition, a healthy coping style increases your trust in your capacity to transition and bounce back.[10] This adaptive approach allows you to face the stressful experience of going through change with less resistance, as you're not putting all your energy into shielding yourself from the experience.

To illustrate how early childhood experiences can affect an adult's coping style, let's look at the story of J.T., a senior administrative assistant in his mid-30s. When I interviewed J.T., he shared that he had spent eight years rehashing a betrayal with a friend.

J.T. grew up in an abusive household where he didn't develop secure attachments with his parents; this shaped his coping style, and he learned not to depend on others to help him feel secure when stressed or overwhelmed.

Over time, he began to avoid stressful situations, abruptly cut off ties with loved ones, and struggled to feel connected to his own emotions. His self-esteem suffered as a result; he would often beat himself up when things in life didn't go well.

After ending a long relationship, J.T. again found himself under stress, and had difficulty managing his emotions and effectively self-soothing. He shared details of the breakup with his co-workers, only to find out that they were all talking to each other about what he was going through when he wasn't around. That breach in trust angered J.T., leading him to start testing them by sharing different versions of a story with them to see what got around.

One of J.T.'s coworkers, Eva, caught on to this and felt betrayed by his attempts to catch people in the act of gossiping. Her resentment lingered over the course of their friendship and negatively affected their interactions. Eight years later, Eva felt he was lying about something and brought up the old incident of him spreading multiple versions of a story around. J.T. had a hard time accepting her accusation and was upset that she was rehashing the past betrayal. After that conversation, he cut off contact with Eva, without involving her in the process. His anger fueled his conviction. His desire to avoid the whole issue got the best of him.

Over the course of our interview, J.T. and I talked about his past experiences of feeling let down by others who weren't there to comfort him in times of pain. He shared the abuse in his home and how hard it was to grow up fearing his father. To cope, he had learned to avoid his own feelings and numb himself to the intensity of emotions that came up in times of conflict or change. This made it harder for him to be in touch with his stress and be able to tune in to his need for self-soothing.

We explored both his pain from childhood and the difficulty Eva had in trusting him. By being present with his emotional experience, he started to understand that it was more than just being angry at Eva harping on an old issue: he was also reacting to past betrayals from childhood.

When J.T. could look at his emotions without judging or minimizing them, he could feel more compassion for what he and Eva were experiencing. This shifted his perception from anger to empathy, and he began to make room for a new ending. Layer by layer, we faced what he had been quick to avoid: having compassion for Eva's experience and his own experience, and understanding that trust was an issue they both wrestled with. Accepting the ways in which he may have let Eva down was hard for him, and brought up shame. But when he found more compassion for her struggle as well as his own, he could approach their situation from a new perspective.

Chapter III

Waving "The Lollipop of Distraction"

"Our destiny is frequently met in
the very paths we take to avoid it."

- Jean de La Fontaine

When there is unresolved hurt from losing an attachment to someone or something you value, you may try to avoid dealing with the hurt in an attempt to just move on. Have you ever told yourself, *It's not that big of a deal* or *Things will blow over with time* or *No need to stir the pot?* I know I have—many times! All of these messages shift your attention away from the discomfort of the hurt, leading you to feel that the problem has vanished. This is what I call waving "the lollipop of distraction," aka: distracting yourself from being present in facing the issue at hand.

Have you ever noticed how a baby in full meltdown state, wailing as if his life is about to be over, becomes instantly mesmerized the minute you wave a big, colorful lollipop in front of him? The defense mechanisms of denial and avoidance are effective lollipops that we use when we get overwhelmed, our sense of self feels threatened, and the intense emotions that come up feel like too much to handle. If you don't know how to effectively self-soothe, avoidance feels like the safest approach to take. But in doing so, you miss the chance to get closure and heal so you can effectively move forward.

Lollipops of distraction can detract your attention from the core pain that got buried through avoidance.

And what happens as you continue avoiding the pain? The present moment gets shaped to reinforce old stories of goodbyes being too painful to face. By avoiding the situation and the emotions it brings up, you reinforce the belief that you can't face change and loss. And so the vicious cycle continues.

In J.T.'s case, the lollipop of distraction included avoidance of the impact of losing his friendship, denying the grief of feeling betrayed by Eva, and being unable to appreciate that she also felt betrayed by him. As a result, their friendship deteriorated.

Once J.T. could get past the tempting distraction of avoidance, he could face what was happening with his friendship without blame, anger, or denial. He began to make room for a more informed decision about how to proceed with Eva—a decision rooted in deeper understanding and compassion.

When you face a moment of change, what you go through becomes magnified and shaped by past memories. Such was the case with Eva, who felt betrayed by J.T. years before when he tested people's trustworthiness. They weren't able to come to healing and closure around that incident, so the wound stayed open. Fast forward to today, when the past pain of feeling betrayed colored her reaction to what was happening between them in the present moment; she thought he was lying about something that he called a misunderstanding.

Though the lollipop of distraction offers immediate relief, it is short-lived. To obtain real resolution, you must face the situation directly. When we dive into The Good Goodbye approach in Part 2 of the book, I'll show you how you can lean on your own resilience to cope with the stress of change and minimize the temptation to avoid it.

Through self-introspection and present awareness, you can connect to your emotions and allow them to be expressed, rather than suppressed. You can learn to tolerate the stress of grief, fear, or other emotions associated with a change or loss. Even acknowledging that you're afraid to face your emotions is a step in the right direction, as you're making room for what scares you. By doing so, you can begin to heal the open wound and move forward without being burdened by unfinished business.

In J.T.'s case, he demonstrated how hard it was to let go and find resolution that allowed for full closure. Rehashing the broken trust between Eva and him over eight years was a clear indication that the ways they tried to find closure weren't working. They both had wounds that were crying out for attention, yet those cries were being muffled by growing resentment and frustration.

During our conversation, I had J.T. explore the matter from Eva's perspective to change the lens through which he was viewing their situation. I was also hoping to get rid of the lollipop of distraction; I wanted him to move to a place of looking at what had unfolded between them without judgment. I wanted him to understand that what was happening wasn't just about the present situation with Eva, but was also a chance to heal wounds from the past.

I asked J.T. what he thought Eva needed by constantly bringing up something—the trust issue—that he had moved on from. And what did he need that Eva couldn't provide, leading him to consider ending the friendship?

J.T. and Eva were facing a conundrum: they didn't have the tools to repair their relationship. Trust was broken. Forgiveness seemed far out of reach.

I reflected to J.T. that when people get very fixated on something in their life that went differently from how they planned, like Eva constantly rehashing J.T.'s breach of trust, it devastates them and keeps them from moving on. When new situations arise that brush up on those old wounds, it's a beautiful opportunity to heal what wasn't healed in the past and what needs healing in the present. In helping J.T. see this opportunity, he was able to get unstuck from feeling things were over between them. Upon seeing the positive opportunity in the situation, J.T. shared,

> *Even something so small can be so heavy on her because she didn't have any people who she could trust in her life growing up. It has affected her as a person. And I didn't even think of that. That's really helpful. I see that'll also help me be more understanding of her, and more patient, as well. I was feeling like I just couldn't do this anymore, that I was tired of the rehashing, so something just clicked and I just wanted to say I'm done!*

When you allow yourself to be present with your emotions and feel compassion for your experience, you can increase your compassion for yourself and others. This in turn allows for deeper healing and an opening of new thoughts and behaviors that can help you cope more effectively. I often relate this to a pendulum shift. The pendulum starts swinging by going to the far right and then to the far left, and then it goes a little less to the right, a little less to the left, until finally it settles in the middle.

J.T. was on one end of the pendulum; he second-guessed himself and put up with the constant rehashing with Eva because he felt he deserved it for breaking her trust. All of a sudden, he realized he didn't want to deal with it anymore. So he kicked the pendulum and it swung to the opposite end, to the extreme response of "I'm done! Out of my life!" This was the polar opposite of where J.T. started, but it also wasn't reflective of where he *wanted* to be.

After learning some tools to put the lollipop of distraction aside and deal with his feelings, J.T. might find that he second-guesses less than he used to. And while he might still feel that quick, reflexive "I'm done, no more!" response, he thinks a little bit more before reacting. Eventually, he'll land in the middle, where he can wholeheartedly trust his capacity to cope with whatever he's facing and look objectively at the scenario before reacting. Before he and I talked, J.T. hadn't thought about his past or Eva's past as connected to their current situation. But once he became aware of it, he could feel hopeful and even consider reaching out to her to create a more positive experience of closure. That's the pendulum settling in the middle.

When your heart opens up through understanding and compassion, you have more access to options.

While you once may have believed that your life toolbox only contained a hammer to nail the door shut and walk away, you now realize there are a number of tools at your disposal.

By recognizing that change and goodbyes are opportunities to heal what's been hurt, not just in the present moment, but also in your past, you have access to more resources that help you heal and move forward with greater ease.

J.T. had a lifetime of heartbreak that was fueling his desire to shut the door on his friendship. But when he was able to look at the situation more objectively and feel deeper compassion for both himself and Eva, his heart was more open to accepting that the opportunity being presented to them was a chance to say goodbye to an eight-year-old dynamic of struggle and resentment, and to heal broken trust. He now had options for how to move forward that he couldn't access earlier when firmly holding on to past beliefs and experiences. He could consciously choose to embrace change with more trust and understanding.

It's tempting to wave the lollipop of distraction to avoid being present with what has changed or with what you have lost as a result of a change. Though it may bring temporary relief, it can also become a chronic pattern of avoidance that will make it harder for you to cope in healthy ways down the road. When you dive into Part 2 of the book and *The Good Goodbye Blueprint*, I'll provide you with exercises to help you practice being present with a change you're facing and the emotions it provokes inside of you. You'll learn to build your capacity to cope with the stress of change. Your increased ability to soothe yourself in healthy ways will give you more room to navigate change with greater compassion and openness to new solutions.

Chapter IV

What's Grief Got to Do with It?

"Live as if you were to die tomorrow.
Learn as if you were to live forever."

-Mahatma Gandhi

As we've discussed, facing change often brings up the fear of losing an attachment to someone or something you value. And if you lose that attachment, you are also facing an ending of what you had.

As a society, we don't embrace change and endings well. To create a new collective story about goodbyes, we need to change how we view change. We need to accept that with every change comes an ending. And that an ending, whether it be of a life, relationship, job, or limiting belief, means a death of its existence in that state.

Death is a topic that frequently gets associated with the ending of someone's life. Dealing with death tends to bring up feelings of pain and suffering, something that we're fearful of. But death surrounds us at every moment. Your body's cells are dying as they are renewing. Nature goes through infinite cycles of birth and death. Relationships come and go. When you start a new chapter in life, the previous one ends.

Death is an unavoidable part of life, yet finding ways to meet it with an openness to saying goodbye remains a challenge. We aren't commonly taught that death is a place for both grief and joy, that endings are beautiful entryways to something new. As a result, it can be easy to avoid dealing with it and view death as a taboo topic. When you avoid what you fear, the fear grows.

When you accept that every change, including the ending of life, is a death and an opening to a new opportunity, you take the charge out of what you fear.

Looking at change as a part of life that everyone faces, rather than a horrible and unacceptable ending you can't get through, will allow you to trust your resilience and invite it in more. This takes practice and faith, especially when you're facing a major change that's rocking your world. But the more you embrace the notion that change, endings, and death are interrelated, the more you can accept their natural, necessary role in your life.

When you go through a change, you face a loss, which triggers a stress response of grief, a natural part of coping with any loss.[11] One of the most well known and widely accepted theories of grieving is Elizabeth Kübler-Ross' five stages of grief, explained in her 1969 book, *On Death and Dying*.[12] The five stages are:

Denial
Anger
Bargaining
Depression
Acceptance

In short, these stages are referred to as DABDA. This model was initially developed to give insight into the series of emotions terminally ill patients go through when facing death. However, Kubler-Ross later expanded the application of these stages to all kinds of loss, not just death. The book received widespread appeal among the general public as a way to help people understand the dynamic, complex nature of the grieving process and how it evolves over time. The stages aren't linear in nature; they can occur in any order, if at all, depending on the person. The ultimate goal is to come to terms with, or accept, the loss.

Grief helps you effectively deal with no longer having an attachment to what you valued. Emotions come up to be expressed and released, giving you room inside to keep moving through the layers of grief. By allowing yourself to experience those emotions as they come in waves, you can eventually soothe yourself back to a place of security and comfort. However, as we talked about earlier, if you don't have the tools to self-soothe, the intensity of your emotions can be frightening and you can be tempted by the lollipop of distraction to avoid dealing with it.

I'm amazed at how little room there is for grief to be expressed when it doesn't involve the death of a person. Take, for example, the workplace. Organizations, just like people, go through stages of change. From startup to closure, an organization is constantly evolving. But how often does that evolution get recognized with permission to grieve? Have you ever been part of a big change at work where you felt there wasn't room to talk about what was happening?

My friend Renee has dealt with constant change throughout her career. As a seasoned specialist in the Silicon Valley technology industry, where company startups, acquisitions, and closures happen frequently, she questioned if a stable job was ever possible.

A few years ago, her company was acquired by another organization. With the acquisition came reorganization of departments and teams; this meant layoffs. Despite her track record of success, Renee was terrified of losing her job. She was saddened to be losing the workplace culture of her company as it adapted to the culture of the new organization. Upper management provided few details, which led to several creative rumors about what was really going on.

Renee tried her best to remain objective, but her anxiety increased. She feared not having enough income to sustain herself if she was laid off, despite having a healthy savings account. She frantically weighed her options to either search for a new job or stay at her current company and risk being out of work. Her anxiety convinced her she'd be losing her job, but she felt too frozen to do anything about it.

Weeks went by with no updates from management. Renee was going through a majority of each day planning for the worst and feeling isolating fear, which traumatized her. The story she told herself during this stressful period concluded that the decision makers were solely focused on the bottom line and didn't care about the people being negatively impacted by the change. She felt increasingly alone in her struggle and couldn't find healthy ways to self-soothe and cope with the stress. She couldn't make room to grieve what she was losing—the previous company culture, her sense of security in having a stable job, and her coworkers who were being laid off.

Ultimately, Renee kept her job and transitioned to a new working culture with the acquiring organization. Relieved, she went about with her job and put the whole traumatic experience out of her mind. She never dealt with the grief of what she lost or the effects of feeling such intense, isolating fear. Yet the story she had created—that she'd lose her job and no one would look out for her best interest—got internalized and stored away.

Fast forward a few years, and Renee's company faced another acquisition. She went through the same pattern of thoughts, emotions, and behaviors that had colored her previous experience. Anxiety. Fear of losing her job. Lack of trust in her employer. The past story became her current reality and she struggled to find a different way to cope with the present change.

One night at dinner, I asked Renee if her company was talking about the emotional impact of being acquired. No, she said. There wasn't room at work for employees to grieve this major transition. There wasn't space for them to voice their concerns or understand why this was happening. Rather, the company leaders were focused on communicating the benefits of the acquisition and celebrating the transition.

Leaders are responsible for shepherding an organizational community through any transition to keep operations functional. But when big changes occur, it can be easy to bypass the grief of what's changed and just focus on maintaining organizational control and productivity. While it's important to see the positive side to a big organizational change, it's equally important to accept what's being lost and make room for the organizational community to grieve alongside the celebration. By doing so, employees are more likely to get on board with the change because they feel supported in their grief and encouraged to make the best out of the situation everyone is facing together.

By allowing yourself to grieve, you create room for all your emotions to be expressed rather than suppressed.

You free yourself from holding on to pain so it doesn't fester inside. With practice, you develop a stronger ability to self-soothe, which gives you more confidence to face any kind of change and trust that you'll move through the experience and come out stronger for it. You learn that while change often brings loss, the grief you feel is part of what will help you heal.

Chapter V

The Impact of Unresolved Loss

"My mother would take the Band-Aid off, clean
the wound, and say, 'Things that are covered
don't heal well.' Mother was right. Things
that are covered do not heal well."

- T.D. Jakes

The loss that comes with change is undeniably going to trigger an influx of emotions, which will be stressful. Ideally, you move through the stress by soothing yourself with what you need to recalibrate: the feelings of protection, comfort, and security. But if you haven't learned how to effectively self-soothe, you can get overwhelmed juggling your emotions and become stuck.[13]

To experience goodbyes in a new way that doesn't set you back, you need to face what's happening without trying to run away from it. I understand that it can be scary and overwhelming to do so, but you must give yourself permission to feel the loss of what's changed and respond with compassionate awareness of what you need to cope. In order to respond to those needs, it's helpful to understand what happens internally when you're faced with loss—there are biological and psychological reasons you feel overwhelmed, out of control, or panicked to the point of holding on for dear life to what has already changed.

Physiologically, myriad reactions occur in your body to manage the stress of change and losing an attachment to someone or something you value. In a matter of seconds, your mind assesses the situation to determine the appropriate response and communicates it to the body for implementation. Blood pressure, breathing rate, hormone levels, muscle contractions, and other stress response mechanisms prepare you for action.[14]

Think about how your body responds when you face a change or loss. Where do you feel the tension or constriction? Do you feel more hungry or not hungry at all? Is there a tightening in your throat or chest? Do you need more or less sleep to cope? By noticing how your body is responding to the stress of change, you can begin to give your body what it needs to manage that stress.

Similarly, you can attend to what happens in your mind when facing change. Your mind becomes busy scanning through files of past experiences to determine how to categorize the present situation. If it's similar to a past one that was painful, your body prepares to respond as though the past pain was occurring right now.[15] Once this happens, you've stepped out of proactively responding to the present and are now reacting to your past.

If you've stored messages or created a story that it's too painful to tolerate change, those messages come to the forefront and skew your perception of your ability to handle the present situation. What gets communicated to your body is, "Protect me from this threat I'm facing; minimize risk to my sense of self."

Your mind starts recording the present situation as both reinforcer of the past and predictor of the future. The story that gets reinforced? Change and goodbyes are threatening and need to be avoided. When you sit in that mind space, you shield yourself from being open to the change. However, if you can shift your perception to prevent the past story you created about goodbyes from being transposed onto the current situation, you can create a new story that better serves you.

I know how hard it is to tolerate the stress and overwhelming emotions when you're in the thick of it. The last thing likely on your mind when going through a change or loss is how to move gracefully through the spectrum of emotions. Instead, you're probably thinking, "How do I survive this without losing my shit?!"

Remember, the goal here is not to minimize or get rid of the grief. You need to feel the grief, and all the emotions that come with it—anger, fear, guilt, sadness, and even relief and gratitude—to heal. You need to give yourself permission to grieve on your own timeframe. It's not a matter of diving into grieving and then being done with it. You'll go through periods of grieving, take breaks from the grief, and eventually find yourself grieving again. But in time, you'll get to the point of not being knocked to the ground by it, and find a new way to more effectively cope with the change or loss.

When you continually avoid grief because you're afraid of feeling it, you end up prolonging your suffering. And conversely, if you stay stuck in grief and avoid feeling emotions on the other end of the emotional spectrum, such as compassion, joy and gratitude, you also complicate your healing process. You prevent yourself from living in the present because your energy is tied up keeping things unresolved. Unresolved endings take up space emotionally, mentally, physically and spiritually, even if you're not conscious of them.

> ## Let the pendulum swing from each end of the emotional spectrum—from grief to gratitude—and then to settle at a place where you feel more at peace with what you've lost.

In my career as a psychotherapist and mental health consultant, I've observed that people's over-reliance on avoidance (of either positive or negative emotions) and inability to effectively manage the stress of change can lead to:

- decreased energy and chronic exhaustion
- increased irritability and frustration
- mental fog and inability to focus
- limiting thoughts and behaviors
- regret about the past, dread of the future, and not fully living in the present
- a lifestyle of chronic stress
- physical pain and illness
- emotional heaviness
- disconnection from or numbness to emotions.

These are just a few ways that unexpressed grief and unresolved loss show up. You may not be sure why you no longer feel as "alive" or connected in life, but you know the brilliant spark that once filled your heart has dimmed to a small glimmer.

To put this into perspective, I want to share the story of Luna, an education professional and business school student in her early 30s. She lost her brother tragically, and was unable to let go of the belief that bad things that happened to her were her fault.

Luna's brother had struggled with depression for many years. Thoughts of dying were not new to him. Luna was a steady support and confidant, someone he would go to in his darkest moments.

One day, he was visiting Luna in her apartment. They briefly caught up on the happenings of the day. Below is Luna's recollection of what happened next:

> *He was sitting at the kitchen table eating, and was deep in thought while looking outside the balcony. We chatted while I was putting my stuff away, then moved our conversation over to the balcony. He asked me if I believed in re-incarnation. I immediately felt his energy shift.*
>
> *He said he was tired of living and wanted to jump right there and then. I encouraged him to go back inside and told him we [would] get him help. So we sat in my bedroom and called up the suicide hotline. I also called the hospital and they said to bring him in to the ER if he was cooperative and if not, to call 911. He was willing to wait for our older brother to come home so we could all go together to the hospital.*

Eventually, he couldn't wait any longer. He got up and opened my bedroom door to get out. I jumped on his back and we were wrestling all the way into the kitchen until we both fell—I was still holding on to his body. He wiggled away by taking off his shirt, ran for the balcony, and jumped. I ran downstairs, but it was too late. He was dead.

Over the next few years, Luna's grief consumed her. She harbored a deep sense of responsibility for her brother's suicide and was plagued with guilt. She replayed the event over and over in her mind, identifying all the steps she should have taken to save him. "It's your fault," she constantly said to herself.

During our interview, I asked about Luna's childhood experiences with change and loss. She shared that growing up, she didn't have a chance to be a child. From the age of four, she was in charge of taking care of her newborn twin siblings. Every year, another sibling would be born and she would be responsible for all of them—seven in total. Her brother who died was the second youngest.

I had to feed them, take care of them, make sure nothing bad happened to them. If any of the kids were misbehaving, it was my fault because I wasn't putting them in their place to act right. If my siblings got beaten up or bullied, it was my fault. I would get told to go do something about it to fix it. I remember at my brother's funeral service, my mom was crying and said "Why didn't you hold him tighter? Why didn't you do more to save him?" When I was talking to my uncle at the service, he said I didn't know how to handle him and that's why he's dead.

The message Luna got from her family was that she was responsible for the livelihood of her siblings and when things didn't go well, it was her fault. This affected Luna throughout her life. It was hard for her to feel at ease, for she always felt the need to keep others happy to avoid being blamed for something going wrong. Luna's situation demonstrates how childhood experiences become engrained in us, taking the form of a story we tell ourselves about who we are and how the world works. When her brother died, she experienced a devastating reenactment of that story.

Her grief about her brother's death was connected to that story. She wanted to let go of it, along with the current belief that she was responsible for her brother's death, but another part of her was strongly identified with the messages her family had reinforced since she was a young child.

I helped Luna see that her journey in grieving the loss of her brother could also be a chance to mourn her childhood experiences of being blamed for her siblings' livelihood. By making room for both current and past experiences of grief, she could start to shift her beliefs and let go of her old story.

I asked Luna if she thought it was possible to have compassion for herself through saying goodbye to her brother and letting go of the belief that she was at fault. She quietly replied that she was still practicing learning how. The part of her that didn't believe she was worthy of love or compassion would need something else to hold onto in order to release the old beliefs:

> *I've felt like I've been chained to something that's been dragging me down for years. Freedom is coming up a lot for me now. I haven't noticed that before, but I'm grateful for it. It helps when I hear other people tell me I did the best I can. Maybe I can learn to let go and move on with my life the way I know my brother would want me to.*

Though Luna's pain will not go away overnight, it was helpful for her to make the connection between her current loss and the old story that was keeping her in a dark space of guilt and remorse. Upon her making that connection, she created room for the possibility of a new interpretation of the loss of her brother, one that freed her from staying stuck in the past so she could create a new life for herself.

Any kind of loss—a life, career, relationship, or dream of a healthy childhood—can be an opportunity to bring to light old wounds so that a more complete healing and closure can occur. You can have a corrective emotional experience, not only for the current change and loss, but also for those past moments that left you stuck and confused, unable and unwilling to move on.

If you allow it, each moment of change can be an entryway into the unhealed parts of your past so you can reconnect to them and move forward with grace.

Chapter VI

The Heart of the Matter

"Only from the heart can you touch the sky."

- Rumi

As your body and mind go into overdrive to protect you from the perceived threat of loss and grief, your heart also goes through its own process. Yet in a society that places more value on the rational, logical interpretations of the mind rather than on the emotional, intuitive experiences of the heart, it's easy to overlook or devalue what's happening in your heart in comparison to your mind.

The purity of grief, of feeling nothing in your heart but the raw emotions of loss associated with a change, is overwhelming. It can trigger you to feel that you're about to explode, break down, or lose your sense of self. However, by allowing yourself to feel your emotions, rather than blocking them, you make room for self-reflection—thinking about and contemplating your unique experience. Self-reflection helps open the doors to understanding and compassion, which are necessary to heal from a change or loss.

Being self-reflective and compassionate is hard to do if you haven't previously learned how and also practiced it regularly. And if you're already feeling discomfort dealing with your mind and body's reactions to the stress of change, getting in touch with the vulnerable rawness of your emotions can scare you into backing away. Do the opposite. Keep feeling your emotions and do your best to understand your experience with compassion.

Connecting to your heart by feeling the rawness of your emotions gives you access to the other healing properties that your heart provides—empathy, wisdom, gratitude, forgiveness and grace are some examples. These expressions of the heart soften your mind's grip on trying to control or rationalize your way through the grief of change. They ignite the courage to face what scares you. They help you get to a place of accepting what you're facing without blame or judgment. Thus, it's important to cultivate your connection with your heart so you can access its healing properties when you need to cope with the stress of change.

Your heart is your healing salve in times of pain.

As researchers become more attuned to human con-sciousness and the ways our mind and body interact, there's increasing evidence that the heart has its own consciousness, and direct influence on your emotions, thoughts, and actions.[16, 17, 18] Your heart influences what the mind perceives and how the body responds. Yet, if your mind's story of goodbyes is so negative that it takes over to divert you from the threat of loss, the heart's emotional and intuitive responses can get quickly tossed to the backseat.

When you feel your raw emotions and respond compas-sionately to your attempts to understand what you're going through, you allow for deep emotional connection to your experience. This helps you move through change. When you're feeling fear, hurt, anger, or any other tough emotion that's triggered by change or loss, it's tempting to want to disconnect from those emotions rather than deepen them. But, as we've seen, disconnec-tion and avoidance as coping strategies complicate mat-ters, making it harder for you to move forward with a sense of closure and completeness.

How often do you tune in to your heart? Are you aware of what your heart needs in times of uncertainty? To find deep healing in life, it's essential that you make room for this kind of connection and understanding. You need to get to the heart of the matter—pun intended.

After going to graduate school to become a clinical psy-chologist, I took a strong interest in the healing arts to understand how to establish a connection with one's heart, including my own. I was tired of feeling overwhelmed by life's challenges and noticed how my desire to detach from my emotions was only making matters worse. I embarked on a 15-year journey of healing where I actively engaged in weekly therapy, spiritual consultations, shamanic healing, alternative medicine practices, and lots of self-care. Learning to deeply reconnect with my emotions and develop compassionate understanding of myself and others required a tremendous amount of patience and curiosity.

Through the wisdom of the therapists and healers with whom I worked, I learned I was disconnected from my heart. They also showed me that if I faced what I was most trying to avoid, I wouldn't break. I wouldn't fall into an abyss of despair when facing life changes. In fact, the opposite would happen. I could thrive.

With dedicated practice, I found more self-compassion, understanding and gratitude for the tough experiences I had throughout life. I could feel the pain of those experiences and forgive myself and others for what I had gone through. In doing so, I healed deep wounds that had filled my heart with sorrow for years. I learned to let go of what had held me back from reaching my full potential, which helped me move forward and accept the lessons from each change and loss as they shaped me into the woman I am today.

I was once incredibly effective in using my mind to rationally power through life's rough waters, but I didn't see how it was holding me back. Now, I can allow myself to dive deep into feeling the rawness of my emotions, feel compassion and love for what I'm going through, and rise up through the process having a more complete appreciation for what I'm experiencing so it can be integrated into my life in a positive manner. Learning to connect to and lead from my heart changed my life. And it will change yours.

Teaching you how to connect to your heart isn't something I would attempt to say I can teach you in this book. As I've learned through my personal healing work, It's a lifelong journey, and your learning will require commitment and focused action each day. However, I recommend you begin the process and learn what you need to develop this connection. In Part 2 of the book and in *The Good Goodbye Blueprint*, I've included exercises that help you connect with your emotions and cultivate self-awareness and compassion.

As you learn to get in touch with your emotions and develop greater understanding of and compassion for your experiences, your confidence and emotional resilience will grow. You will have more trust in your ability to get through tough times without drowning. Self-doubt, fear, and judgment will keep coming up—that's just a part of life. Your mind will continue trying to protect you from what it identifies as threats, including those tough emotions of grief. But when this happens, you can rely on your soothing grace and wisdom to help you get back up when crushed. You can train your heart and mind to work in sync so you can move forward with clarity and purpose.

As you reflect on your own experiences, can you recall times when it was hard for you to feel your emotions? Did you try to 'hold it all together' for fear that if you let your emotions out, they would drown you? It's hard enough to figure out how to cope with a change or loss, let alone deal with the tough emotions that come up. But when you avoid your emotions and don't allow yourself to feel compassion for your experience, you leave your heart out of the picture. When you do this, you complicate your grief and become vulnerable to experiencing the effects of unresolved loss that we discussed earlier (page 49). Your quality of life is affected, and it's harder to find joy in the present or hope for the future.[19]

I have a personal story to illustrate this. At my grandmother's funeral, I ran into a longtime family friend whom I hadn't seen in several years. I was struck by how exhausted he looked. He greeted me with a comfortingly warm smile, but behind his eyes I saw a sorrow and longing that rattled my core.

He shared how he still hadn't accepted his father's suicide and couldn't say goodbye, even though it had been close to 15 years since his father died. His face was filled with accumulated sorrow. He just couldn't move on.

As we talked about the pain of death and the hardship that comes with loss, I kept asking myself, "Why? Why couldn't he accept his father's death? What's happened to him as a result? What would happen if he did accept it?" I felt how those several years of life without accepting the loss of his father had filled his heart with regret and sorrow. And this is where he stayed stuck.

During our conversation, I sensed that while he felt the intensity of grief for years, he couldn't move past it to feel gratitude and compassion for what he had gone through. Had he forgiven himself for any feelings he had that he could have prevented his father's suicide? Did he forgive his father for leaving? I wondered if he felt trapped in despair to avoid feeling compassion and love toward himself. As a result, he'd be unable to reach a deeper level of accepting that although his father chose to end his life in a tragic manner, it had nothing to do with the love he had for his son.

When you continually struggle to cope with a major change or loss, and feel your heart heavy with certain emotions that make it hard to move on, it's important to recognize that you may need additional support to feel other emotions in your heart that can help you heal. Your heart can provide the love, empathy, wisdom, and compassion you need to tend to those tough, even debilitating, emotions. By obtaining the support of a professional counselor, therapist, or healer who is skilled in working with matters of complicated grief and unresolved loss, you can learn how to get unstuck, open your heart to feeling all the emotions from grief to joy, and establish a new way of living with the change and loss that doesn't keep you bound in suffering.

In time, and with dedication to your personal healing, you will learn that even if goodbyes bring heartbreak and pain as you face the unknown territory of change, you can get through them. You will come to understand that grieving what you're losing is a natural, healthy process; if you can move through the process with less resistance and greater care, mercy, and gentleness, you can experience deep transformation and healing.

By getting to the heart of change and loss and feeling the full emotional spectrum—from grief to gratitude—you clear the way for creating an experience that honors everything you're going through. You put the lollipops of distraction to the side and bravely face what's in front of you. You create room to weave the experience into a story that propels you forward in life. This is the precursor to creating a Good Goodbye.

II.

THE GOOD GOODBYE APPROACH

"

When you change the way you look at things, the things you look at change.

— Max Planck

Chapter VII

The Five Pillars

"The secret of change is to focus all of your energy,
not on fighting the old, but on building the new."

-Dan Millman

What does it take to turn the spotlight on another path that can provide healing and empowerment in times of change? What's needed to give people permission to not recreate the past? How do you find the "good" in good-bye?

Over years of supporting people in navigating change using the Kubler-Ross model (DABDA) as a guiding compass, I found myself contemplating a new approach that reflected the gift my mom gave me when she died. The idea was simple: Start with acceptance, and the rest of the process will unfold with more ease.

When you begin with acceptance, you release yourself from putting energy into resisting what's changed.

This frees you up to approach change with more awareness and appreciation. You give yourself the ability to consciously shape your story moving forward, rather than reacting to an old script of what should happen.

The Good Goodbye approach helps you rewrite your narrative around goodbyes. It's a framework for navigating change with empowerment so you learn to embrace rather than fear change. It allows you to bridge the gap from where you are to where you want to be, and take focused action to positively integrate change and loss into your life.

The following five actions are the pillars of The Good Goodbye approach. They are reflective of what people want to experience when dealing with change and loss, as identified through the survey I conducted and my years of professional experience, research, and observation. They include the following (whenever I specifically refer to them throughout the book, I've capitalized them):

THE GOOD GOODBYE APPROACH

Acceptance

Accept the situation without trying to change it or your life story.

Understanding

Deepen your understanding of your existing experience and determine your desired outcome.

Gratitude

Cultivate appreciation for your experience and identify how it can be positively worked into your life.

Forgiveness

Take steps to let go of any resentment, need for retribution, or self-blame that's keeping you stuck.

Saying Goodbye

Integrate Acceptance, Understanding, Gratitude, and Forgiveness into a holistic story that helps you carry out your intention of having a Good Goodbye experience.

As I shared at the beginning of the book, these actions are not intended to be prescriptive or rigidly adhered to and they may not be the only things you'll experience when going through a change or loss. You will find your own process of dealing with the stress of change based on your unique coping style and past experiences with goodbyes. You may not go through each action in the order listed or even need an action. That's okay. Don't look at this approach as an absolute, must-do list to create a new goodbye experience. Rather, use it as a starting point and guide for how to use change to foster greater self-awareness, resilience, and compassion for your experience, and obtain closure by intentionally honoring what's ending so you can be open to a new beginning.

As you adjust to a change or loss and move forward in life, you'll find that there will be reminders of your loss and what has changed—holidays and anniversaries can feel especially poignant and painful. At that point in time, you may want to revisit these actions and see how your story of goodbyes can be updated. Perhaps later down the line you'll feel more Gratitude for your loss, or need to dive deeper into Understanding why it happened. Or you may find that you are still struggling to Accept what's changed. You can refer back to The Good Goodbye actions and choose which one you most need in the moment.

Let's dive into each of the five actions of The Good Goodbye approach.

Chapter VIII

Acceptance

"God, grant me the serenity to accept the things I cannot change, courage to change the things I can, and wisdom to know the difference."

–Reinhold Niebuhr

It's often believed that acceptance is the final step in grieving a change or loss. Some people think that once you accept, you're at the end of the grieving process. This isn't always the case. Grieving is a lifelong process that evolves over time. And acceptance doesn't have to be the last step.

In disciplines such as addiction psychology and Buddhism, acceptance is the first underlying principle from which healing comes. Acceptance and Commitment therapy, used to treat depression, anxiety, and other psychological disorders, teaches clients to accept what's out of their control and then to take action that enriches their lives.[20] Buddhism's first noble truth, "All life is suffering," invites followers to first accept that suffering is a natural part of life in order to live in accordance with that truth.[21] In addiction therapy, once you accept you're an addict, you then take steps to heal the addiction.[22]

In The Good Goodbye approach, Acceptance means you recognize what's happening for you without trying to change, deny, or resist what has happened. By doing that, you save yourself from investing your energy in trying to make something different than what has already transpired. You understand certain things are out of your control, and focus instead on facing your circumstances and using your resources to change and heal what is within your control.

Acceptance doesn't mean you have resolved the hurt or grief that comes up with a change or loss. It doesn't mean you won't go through those difficult emotions of sadness, anger, or anxiety. Remember, grieving is a natural part of how you cope with the loss of an attachment, so it will be part of what you need to heal.

Acceptance is a starting point to acknowledge what has unfolded rather than trying to change reality into something it is not.

Acceptance is a *very* big step, especially when you don't like how things have changed. And it may take a lot of time just to get to that point. But when you practice getting to Acceptance first, the rest of your journey will change. You'll have more space to create a future that's open to any possibility because you're not bound to the past being the only option you can recreate. You can choose how you move forward through the transition to create a story that serves your highest good.

Be careful not to confuse Acceptance with giving up, condoning, or resigning yourself to what has changed that you deem undesirable. Acceptance doesn't mean any of these—in fact, it's quite the opposite. Acceptance requires a strong commitment to put aside what you think *should* be happening, look clearly at what *is* unfolding, and intentionally choose how you want to move through the experience to uphold what's most important to you.

Being mindful enough to look objectively at a change that you're struggling with takes a lot of energy. And remember, when you're facing a change, it triggers a natural stress response that affects your body, mind, and heart. As we discussed earlier, it's important to become familiar with how you cope in times of change and what you need to self-soothe so you can manage the associated stress. The same applies to taking the action of Acceptance.

Focus on responding to any stress by doing what you need to feel as secure, comforted, and protected as possible. Ease your mind of needing to figure everything out all at once or control what's going to happen next. Give your body a lot of rest and replenishment to flush out the influx of stress hormones so they don't build up and lead to physical pain or illness. Practice being compassionate toward yourself. And if it feels like too much to handle, receive the support of others you trust—loved ones, a confidant, therapist, counselor, or healer—to assist you in Accepting what's changed in your life.

Getting to Acceptance is often difficult, and it can bring up old, seemingly unrelated wounds from past goodbyes. However, as you are managing the stress of the change or loss at hand, Acceptance can also jumpstart healing of those old wounds. To illustrate this, let's look at Veronica's story.

Veronica was a 37-year-old therapist. She had her master's degree in counseling psychology and a thriving professional life, and was well on her way to having the life she dreamed of. The only missing piece was a lifelong partner. She deeply longed to get married.

When she started dating a new boyfriend, she believed she'd found the man of her dreams. Things between them blossomed effortlessly. He said all the things she wanted to hear. When they had fights, Veronica wrote them off; she thought they just needed to work harder to become more understanding and tolerant of each other. Typical relationship stuff.

Yet on some occasions, Veronica's boyfriend would get really drunk and angry. In his rage, he would throw things and blame his behavior on Veronica. He would belittle her and accuse her of having low self-esteem. She knew he was putting her down to feel better about himself. But she was too invested in having her dream of getting married come true; she let him continue to manipulate her.

During one argument, he was intoxicated and became particularly hostile and scary. Veronica was in her car getting ready to drive away when he reached through the window and punched her in the mouth. "I was more stunned than the physical pain. I thought to myself, 'Oh my god, I'm in one of those physical abuse relationships. How did I get here?' The hope that I would have the boyfriend that I always wanted kept me going on with him. It was not a rational thought."

Despite being physically attacked, Veronica remained in the relationship. The dream of marriage, along with the intense fear about things having gone terribly wrong, kept her stuck. "I wasn't prepared to handle the grief of the loss of our relationship."

I asked Veronica about the internal process she went through to decide to stay in the relationship.

I was so disconnected from myself. I didn't know myself. The Veronica I know today, she didn't exist. She was buried somewhere because there was this part of me that wanted to make it work, that wanted to ignore things were bad.

Now that I'm thinking about it more, I'm hearing you reflect back that there was this dream I had of getting married that I didn't want to give up. I was fully supporting him while I worked and paid the bills, and this was all in the hopes of him changing. It was me actually trying to make him into someone he was never going to be. He was an alcoholic who had his own work to do which was beyond anything I could do for him. But I completely disregarded that we were worlds apart in terms of ambition, coping skills, and achievement.

At the same time, there was also the grief about ending the relationship, telling people I had ended things when everyone was getting married around me and I was 37. I didn't want to believe this was me and didn't want to accept it.

For me, if the relationship didn't work, it meant I was unlovable, that I couldn't make relationships work. That something was wrong with me. Why wasn't I finding a partner? And it would mean that I was alone. That's the worst thing in the world. Then I'd have to focus on myself and look at all those things that had led me to settle for a terrible, abusive relationship. There was no self-love there. I defined myself by holding on to a partner and have someone [to] distract me. I couldn't handle not having a job, not having a boyfriend. Things were not good. I didn't know what was going to happen.

Veronica was initially unable to take the action of Acceptance. She denied what was happening in order to hold on to an old dream, even at the expense of her physical safety. It took over a year for her to get to a point where she not only Accepted that she was in an abusive relationship, but also acknowledged the ways in which self-love was missing.

Veronica started to get sick and depressed. Her body was hurting a lot. One morning, she couldn't get out of bed. She went to the doctor and learned that she had hypothyroidism and would need ongoing medical treatment. "I had ignored and avoided myself - further evidence I was not in a space where I valued myself enough to listen to my own body telling me, practically yelling, I was sick."

The walls were closing in on what she was doing emotionally. She couldn't keep avoiding what was clearly facing her: it was time to say goodbye to the relationship. "I was so scared to do it. My body had to take over and do the breakup for me. It was traumatizing. Heart palpitations, short[ness] of breath. I waited until the last minute when I could not tolerate it anymore physically, emotionally, and intellectually. But I did it and told him that he needed to call his parents to get him to move out. And so we said goodbye."

As a therapist, Veronica had an analytical understanding of what she was going through, but her heart was broken. Her pattern of denial during the relationship had led her to detach from her own heart, and she didn't know how to process the emotions she was feeling. She had been holding on so tightly to her dream of finding "the one." Now she was at a crossroads. She could continue holding onto that dream, or she could choose to let it go and create a new goodbye story. She chose to let it go.

Saying goodbye—letting go—was hard, because it made Veronica face herself and the ways she'd been living detached from herself. In the end, not only did Veronica get herself out of an abusive relationship, but she also gained insight into her history and began to heal old wounds.

*I remember telling my boyfriend when we first
met that there was something we were meant*

to learn from each other. For me, it opened up a huge door. As fucked up as the relationship was, I can't help but feel gratitude for the power within me to see there was so much I was trying to avoid, to see how the Veronica that's here today was so buried. But now I'm so grateful she's here with me because she's pretty fucking great. I fell in love with myself a little bit more. It's a pretty wonderful feeling.

Veronica's wounds were rooted in her long-held belief that she was unlovable. When she found the strength to end her abusive relationship, she gave herself a chance to heal those wounds. She began to Accept the reality of being abused and lacking love for herself. She acknowledged her desire to be free of past stories of un-worthiness that held her back, and she opened herself up to heal what had prevented her from fully experiencing aliveness in her heart.

As you think about Veronica's story, can you relate to her experiences? Were there times when you struggled to Accept what you were facing, even if it meant that in doing so, you would experience more hurt? To practice Acceptance in your life, pay attention to what you're facing right now; don't try and change it. If past stories of how things should be come up, recognize the thoughts, but don't let them reenact themselves as you respond to the situation. You don't have to agree with what has happened, or fear that by Accepting it, you're condoning something or someone that hurt you. Try and tolerate being present with it, without judgment. A goodbye moment is unfolding. If you can simply acknowledge that, you can direct your energy to move through the process of an empowered letting go.

There are exercises in *The Good Goodbye Blueprint* to help you with the action of Acceptance. Once you're done reading the book, complete the exercises to start creating your own Good Goodbye.

Chapter IX

Understanding

"Between stimulus and response there is a space. In that space is our power to choose our response. In our response lies our growth and our freedom."

- Victor Frankl

When you Accept change, you increase your capacity to respond to the present situation more clearly. Acceptance also helps you acknowledge your past, face the present, and be open to an unknown future. The space between where you are right now and where you will go next can be huge. And it can feel especially terrifying if you don't know where you want to go next.

We spend an incredible amount of energy trying to predict our future; it helps us feel a sense of control, because uncertainty is scary.[23] Out of anxiety and fear, we may convince ourselves that the past is going to repeat in the future—and this becomes a self-fulfilling prophecy. We echo old patterns, close ourselves off to new experiences, stop growing, and miss out on life itself.

But the space between where you are and where you want to be is where the magic happens. This is where you create the story of your life. You get to select what beliefs, thoughts, and actions you want to take with you to keep moving forward, and decide what you're ready to leave behind. In order to make this leap, you need to know what you desire as an outcome from the change or loss you're facing, and feel secure enough to tolerate a new experience. And this is what the second action, Understanding, is about: Deepen your understanding of your existing experience and determine your desired outcome.

Understanding—specifically through self-reflection—helps you assess the value your existing goodbye story and beliefs bring to creating the kind of goodbye you desire. It gives you a means of correcting inaccurate thoughts or behaviors that are causing you hardship.[24] To evolve, you need to continually and critically assess and reassess how you're making meaning of the world and determine if what you've learned in the past still applies to the present. This self-reflection helps you become an active participant in shaping your life, rather than going through each day on autopilot.

The action of Understanding requires you to be mindful of your thoughts and discern which ones are limiting you from a new experience (based on fears, old stories, or irrational beliefs), and which ones reflect what you truly desire. You also need to develop insight into what you're facing that's been hard for you to look at until now.

Remember that your mind is conditioned to keep you away from perceived danger and to maintain a sense of control. If, based on your past experiences, you've reinforced that change and goodbyes are painful, your mind is going to do its best to keep you away from them. To allow for a new experience, you must learn to create and nurture new thoughts that are aligned with your desires so they grow stronger. As you do this, your mind will start to identify new ideas, opportunities, thoughts, and actions that can support making those desires reality.[25]

Understanding involves the following four steps:

Identify your current emotional experience.

In Accepting what you're facing, how do you feel? What emotional triggers or past goodbye stories are coming up that make it hard to be open to a new experience? What are you disappointed by? What didn't go the way you wanted?

Assess how your past goodbye experiences are influencing the current situation.

What beliefs or stories do you have about what good-byes mean based on past experiences? How are they influencing your perception of what you're currently facing? In what ways is your story holding you back? What fears are playing a role in you not letting go of what's changed?

Determine how you'd like to move forward.

How do you want to feel about yourself, others, and what you're saying goodbye to as you move through the change or loss? Are you committed to releasing your grip on the past and openly facing the unknown future? How would you like to come out of this experience on the other side?

Define what you need in order to stay open to a new experience.

What do you need to self-soothe and manage the natural stress response of grief to get back to an internal sense of security, comfort, and protection? Can you identify examples of how you've overcome change in the past to remind you of your resilience? What motivators or support do you need to stay the course?

The action of Understanding allows you to consider how you want to bridge the gap from where you are to where you want to be as you move through a change or loss. Ask yourself, *Do I want to get through it with openness to learning? Am I wanting to feel compassion for myself and others? Do I want to find forgiveness through the experience?* Whatever you identify as important for you to experience as you go through the transition will influence the subsequent actions you take.

Take the time to work through the four steps of Understanding and complete the exercises in *The Good Goodbye Blueprint* to set the intention that your desires will guide you through this experience. Practice being patient with yourself and go at the pace that feels right to you. Make room for all your thoughts and emotions to emerge in response to the change or loss, whatever they may be.

Remember what I went through when my mom died? Some would have said that the last thing I should have felt was joy during her funeral, but that's exactly what my heart felt—right there next to the heartbreaking grief.

Give yourself room for all your feelings to have a voice without judging if they are appropriate or not.

Practice recognizing where those feelings are coming from. This will help you connect to and be guided by your heart's desires.

As you sift through your feelings, decide which ones you want to feel more of. Sadness? Anger? Gratitude? Forgiveness? Chances are, you'll want to feel more positive emotions. Focus on those and let yourself be guided by them; as a result, you'll find more compassion and appreciation for your experience, which will lead to more compassion and appreciation for others and for the situation you're going through. When you develop a holistic Understanding of your situation, you free yourself from staying stuck in one emotional state, and can direct your energy to walk toward your desired outcome.

Understanding can also help get you through the goodbyes in life that haven't happened yet—perhaps things you're having a hard time letting go of, even though you know you need to, to change your situation for the better. By actively reflecting on what's going on in your life and deciding how you want to feel moving forward, you step into a place of power: you can address these good-byes head-on. Joseph's story is a prime example of that.

Joseph was a senior executive in his mid 50s who had been with his current company for 15 years. He was a stellar performer who had worked all over the world, bringing his expertise to benefit countless organizations and employees—in short, the type of employee that any company would hire in a heartbeat.

But when I spoke with him, he was completely burned out, and running on fumes. For the past *four years*, he'd been dreading showing up to the office each day. His weekends were full of work that he couldn't do during the week because there was just too much to fit into a 24-hour day. Sound familiar? I know I've been there!

Joseph knew he couldn't tolerate a life of burnout, but he didn't know what to do to change his situation. He tried for years to change his attitude about his job, telling himself, "It's probably the same at any other company, so I should just stay where I am."

A small part of him believed that things would one day change. But they didn't. Over time, he got more and more depleted. But because he was such a high achiever, it was hardly noticeable to anyone else at work. He kept getting praise for his work and asked to take on more projects. He kept saying yes.

I saw an opportunity for Joseph to use the action of Understanding to help him end the years of burnout in his career. I started by having him identify his existing experience. Joseph talked through all the reasons he became so unhappy at work. He shared that he didn't feel valued and appreciated. He was exhausted, unhappy, and cynical about his future. Next, I had Joseph describe his desired outcome: Having a career where he had more flexibility and freedom to create his daily schedule. More time to mentor future leaders. Space in his week to write more and do more research. A life with more balance, satisfaction, and joy.

He'd been burned out for four years. When I asked him if he could put in another four years of going through the motions, he responded with an emphatic "No!" How about two years? Same response. One year? Joseph adamantly stated that he would only tolerate nine more months of this state. Nine months! Joseph now had a timeline in place from which to take focused action.

To help Joseph Understand more fully what was keeping him stuck, we peered into the gap in between where he was and where he wanted to be. He acknowledged that he hadn't left his job because he was afraid of not having another job to go to. He was afraid to be in a place where he didn't know what his life would look like. Simply put, he feared the unknown and saying goodbye to something—even if it was draining his energy—without a solid plan in place for where he would head next.

As we dove deeper into the gap, Joseph revealed a deep fear of running out of money and being poor. In his mind, if he left his job and didn't get hired somewhere else, he'd be broke. He had two kids, a mortgage, and a comfortable lifestyle. To have that threatened would be falling into a metaphorical abyss. He was so scared of this possibility that it kept him from taking action or even creating a solid vision that allowed for a different outcome: walking safely across the gap to the other side.

When we explored his past stories surrounding this fear, Joseph shared that he had grown up in a lower middle-class family where finances were a constant source of tension. He hated seeing his family deal with the ongoing stress of not having any money. To prevent himself from repeating what he feared, he stayed stuck in his job and put up with the burnout and unhappiness. This seemed a better approach than going back to that childhood place of pain.

Through the action of Understanding, Joseph identified his existing experience, desired outcome, and the grief that existed in facing an uncertain future. He realized the need to give up an attachment to an old story that protected him from revisiting his past. His goodbye opportunity wasn't just leaving his unsatisfying job, but letting go of an old fear of being poor.

Joseph walked away with a deeper appreciation of how his past stories were getting in the way of him creating a new outcome, and a life free of burnout. He had greater compassion for his experience and how his childhood pain was still with him as an adult. He was now more Accepting of his situation and ready to create a goodbye experience that would propel him forward in a different way.

Some weeks after our interview, I got an email from Joseph. He had met with his supervisor and informed her that he would be stepping out of his current position in nine months—the exact amount of time he'd told me he could continue tolerating his current state! He didn't know how she would respond. But based on what he desired, he faced the unknown and declared his needs. And in doing so, he began creating the bridge to get him to the place where he could make his desired outcome a reality.

To his surprise, Joseph's supervisor worked with him to create an action plan to support his transition. She was open to discussions about what he could still do at the company that would give him more space to create a balanced life. Joseph also opened himself up to exploring new opportunities outside of his company. And he also started devoting more time on the weekends to do things that bring him joy, as well as traveling more for enjoyment, rather than just for work.

Joseph had put a plan of action in place, and in doing so, he began to believe that there was an end in sight. Even if he didn't know what exactly he'd be doing in the future to pay his bills, he found he was more trusting that whatever unfolded would be in alignment with his desire to create a life he loved. This was a positive experience for Joseph's company as well. Rather than having him explode one day from burnout and quit on the spot, they got a chance to participate in a Good Goodbye with him and help create a more fulfilling chapter in his career.

Understanding requires a lot of self-reflection and curiosity about how you're dealing with a situation. This means paying close attention to your thoughts and feelings; noticing how your body copes with the stress of change; and identifying your true desires. Successfully getting through Understanding is dependent on you getting to the heart of the matter: identifying the core issues and emotions that play a big role in how you experience change and loss, and courageously facing what scares you and has kept you stuck in the past.

As you Understand the factors that influence how you're viewing the situation, you can extend your Understanding to others and the situation as a whole. You can start experiencing Gratitude for the experience—the next action in The Good Goodbye approach.

Chapter X

Gratitude

"The most complete and true happiness comes in moments, when you feel right there, completely present, with no ideas about good and bad, right and wrong - just a sense of open heart and open mind."

—Pema Chodron

As discussed earlier, your life is comprised of a series of stories about who you are and how things work in the world based on your perception and interpretation of events—and these stories influence how you interpret future situations. The power of your story is immense. If you aren't aware of how your perspective and interpretations shape your future, you limit room for a new type of experience, and the past tends to repeats itself.[26, 27]

When you seek to create a story that highlights the good in a goodbye moment, you aren't forced to repeat negative patterns that keep you from getting to a place of closure. You take what you've learned and actively choose what thoughts, emotions, and behaviors will most support you as you move forward. Think about J.T.'s story: once he reflected on how both he and Eva were trying to heal past hurts of betrayal and broken trust, he could choose to be more compassionate and move forward in a positive way.

The third action of Gratitude involves cultivating appreciation for the situation you're facing and identifying how it can be positively worked into your life. When you're going through a change that you perceive as negative, it's extremely hard to be appreciative for it. You're hurting, and dealing with the stress of losing what's changed. You may feel that you've been wronged or are being punished, and by being grateful, you'd be condoning whatever or whoever has hurt you. But just as we discussed when it came to Acceptance, having Gratitude does not mean you have to like or agree with the change.

By Accepting what you're facing and Understanding how you want to get through the change, you've done a lot of work to free yourself of being bound to an old goodbye story. You can now devote your energy to experiencing the emotions that uplift you. Remember that survey I conducted where people talked about their feelings around goodbyes? Well, gratitude was the number one emotion survey respondents *wanted* to experience when it came to goodbyes. More than Acceptance or Forgiveness or Understanding, they wanted to get to a place of feeling grateful for the experience, even if it was painful.

When you experience a change, it's easy to focus on and yearn for what you've lost. But if you stay in this space of wanting what you don't have, you aren't able to fully appreciate what's in your life in the present moment. You can get stuck clinging to the past, which can complicate your coping process.

Gratitude gets you out of staying stuck at the grief end of the emotional spectrum. It shifts your perception from what you lost to what you gained. It gives you an objective view of your experience so you can learn, heal, and deepen your appreciation for what you're going through. And going forward, Gratitude will help you more easily Accept and Understand the challenges you face in the future. When you cultivate Gratitude on a regular basis, you increase your quality of life and well-being, not to mention reduce stress, experience more positive emotions, and become more resilient to navigating changes in life.[28, 29]

If you've gone through any sort of loss, you probably know firsthand that Gratitude can seem very out of reach when you're in the midst of pain. This is a sign that at that moment, you're needing to work through the stress reaction of grief. Let it be that way. Do your best to take care of your mind, body, and heart at your own pace and on your own timeframe. Gratitude has a place here, though.

As you move through a wave of grief, you can self-soothe by incorporating Gratitude. This can be as simple as taking a few minutes each day to write out all your raw thoughts and emotions about a change you're struggling to cope with. After you're done writing, take a short break and attend to the emotions that came up. Later that evening or the next morning, re-read what you wrote and identify what you're grateful for and appreciate about the experience you wrote about. Allow your appreciation to positively shift your thoughts, even if just for a moment, so you can keep identifying more of what you appreciate in your life right now. Do this exercise each day, and in time, your mind will be conditioned to make room for Gratitude along with grief.

In my work as a psychotherapist, I found that people who struggled to get to a place of Gratitude were also struggling with letting go of old stories of feeling wronged or punished. Gratitude felt like a simplistic gesture that would mask their pain. What they learned through our work is Gratitude is instead a dedicated practice of objectively identifying the opportunities that exist for you to grow and heal from past negative beliefs or experiences. Gratitude frees you from holding on to suffering that harms your mind, body, and heart.

Cultivating Gratitude is less challenging when you've worked to Accept and Understand a situation from a holistic perspective. When you continually practice self-reflection and deepen awareness of who you are, what past stories influence you, and how you want to show up to new experiences, you can more easily access Gratitude to develop an integrated perspective and story of a goodbye experience. Think of Gratitude as a centering mantra that you call upon to get out of a stuck space of negativity. When you're in the thick of it, the last thing you're conditioned to do is calmly reach for that mantra. But by practicing it over and over, especially as a way of living, it will be easier for you to access when you most need it.

Though many books teach you how to be more grateful in your life, I want to focus here on how you can foster Gratitude within The Good Goodbye framework by practicing presence and compassion. This will also prepare you for the fourth action of The Good Goodbye approach: Forgiveness.

Gratitude and Forgiveness are very closely intertwined.

As you experience more Gratitude, you'll be more open to Forgiveness. As you Forgive, you'll be more Grateful for your experience.

Let's first dive into how to cultivate Gratitude through increased presence and compassion. *The Good Goodbye Blueprint* also has exercises to help you with this.

PRESENCE

To practice presence as a way to increase Gratitude, start by either writing down or saying to yourself, *Right now, I'm grateful for (fill in the blank)*. Take your time to identify anything that you appreciate and are thankful for at this very moment. Notice how easy or hard it is for you to answer this question. Seek to find more things that you're grateful for, no matter how small or insignificant they may seem. The goal is to get your mind to generate positive thoughts to counterbalance any negative thinking. You've now taken stock of your blessings and shifted your perspective from lack (what you've lost or don't have) to abundance (what you do have).

Next, bring your attention to the change you're facing, or what's hard for you right now. Reflect on how you're coping with that change. While you do this, try to keep from judging or criticizing yourself or the situation. We'll touch on how to do this more in the section about compassion below.

Pay attention to the thoughts going through your mind, the physical sensations of your body, and the emotions in your heart. Ask yourself, *What's been getting in the way of me making my desires to experience a Good Goodbye a reality?* By asking this question, you can start exploring what might have been hard for you to learn, get over, or heal. You're taking this moment to reflect on your life journey up to this point. In doing this, you're not living in the past, but being present right now with how the past has affected you.

When you recognize what's been hard for you up until this point, you can soften into appreciating what you're going through.

As you sift through the difficult feelings and thoughts you have about the situation, ask yourself, What one thing am I grateful for amidst this struggle? What is one blessing I can appreciate receiving as a result of this change or loss? No matter what you identify—it may be gratitude that you can actually feel your emotions, or gratitude that you have the security of a roof over your head and food to eat—let this be a starting place of expanding your awareness of what you appreciate and are thankful for in the present moment as you cope.

When you focus your attention on the present moment and take inventory of what blessings you have right now, you actively teach your mind to expand its focus beyond the negative. This takes practice, as your mind is naturally conditioned to zoom in on what's not working, what you don't have, and what it perceives as threats to your well-being. But the more you work on Gratitude, the more you'll be able to perceive your situation through a new lens: one that includes identifying the good in what you're facing.

COMPASSION

Another way to foster Gratitude is through compassion. Compassion is a thread that weaves through all the actions of The Good Goodbye approach, mainly because it both helps you self-soothe, and helps you avoid victimhood or self-blame. Yet compassion can be incredibly hard to access when you're dealing with the stress of change and loss.

Soothing yourself by doing what helps you feel more at ease and less stressed is a form of self-compassion. So is taking care to not be judgmental, critical, or harsh toward yourself. This may mean engaging in some not-so-healthy behaviors or actively avoiding dealing with things for a while. Think about those times you dove into a carton of ice cream after a breakup, or had one too many glasses of wine after a stressful day at work. A bit of this is okay, as it helps you regulate your stress response in the near term. But remember, when you over-invest in avoidance or denial, you set yourself up for complicating your coping process in the long run.

To cultivate compassion, you need to make room for your emotional experience without trying to minimize, downplay, or get rid of any part of what you're dealing with.

Try to comprehend your experience without judgment, criticism, or self-punishment. By allowing your experience to be what it is, you give room for all your emotions to be expressed. This releases the charge from them. In turn, you also create space to release any feelings that you were wronged, misunderstood, or abandoned.

As you experience compassion for your situation, you can introduce the element of Gratitude. Ask yourself, What was hard or hurtful about what I went through? What did I wish happened that didn't? What do I appreciate about myself in having faced this change? What have I gained as a result of this experience that I didn't have before? As you begin appreciating what you went through with more compassionate eyes, it gives you the capacity to extend your compassion to others and feel empathy for what we are all facing when we Say Goodbye.

Why is extending compassion and empathy important? It gives you a fuller picture of the situation. Learning to have empathy means you consciously work to understand someone's experience without judgment—putting yourself in their shoes to feel what they're feeling. How do you do this when you feel that someone else has hurt you or contributed to your loss? Compassion and presence. You can foster Gratitude for another person and the situation you went through by trying to comprehend what they were going through that made them engage in actions that were hurtful. What needs did they have that they were struggling to meet in a healthy way? What can you appreciate about that person and the role they had in your life? Can you feel any love and compassion toward them?

When you step outside of your experience to envision what another person's experience is like, you make room for deeper appreciation of the situation you were both involved with. As you do this, you free up your energy and emotional ties to your struggle and can redirect that energy toward creating what you desire most to have a Good Goodbye. Later on, I'll share the story of Sara, who used Gratitude to cope with a tragic loss and empower herself to start a new chapter in life.

Chapter XI

Forgiveness

"True forgiveness is when you can say,
'Thank you for that experience.'"

-Oprah Winfrey

The fourth action in The Good Goodbye approach is Forgiveness. This action involves taking steps to let go of any resentment, need for retribution, or self-blame that's keeping you stuck. Like Gratitude, Forgiveness may feel impossible to access when you're in the midst of a change or loss. And even if you're years past a difficult goodbye that you can't move on from, chances are a big part of what's kept you stuck is your inability to Forgive—whether it's yourself, another person, or the situation.

I know I've said this multiple times, but it's important to reiterate: Give yourself time and space to get here. You'll be ready when you're ready. Perhaps your unique situation doesn't require Forgiveness. But if it does, use this book and *The Good Goodbye Blueprint* as a framework to shift your perception of what's possible for you, and practice getting to that place you desire with continual focus and dedication.

It's also important to recognize that Forgiveness isn't an easy act that involves saying some simple words and magically, everything is healed. It's a constant practice of expressing your hurt and pain; understanding what you can learn from the situation; releasing yourself, another person, or the situation from ongoing resentment or anger; and rebuilding yourself to move forward with compassion and appreciation. You may Forgive, then find a new wave of hurt, resentment or anger come up. Take time to work through that wave, then revisit the action of Forgiveness again.

I also want to reiterate that Forgiveness doesn't have to mean acquiescence or approval of a hurtful action. Forgiving someone isn't the same as condoning what a person did. Rather, it's a means of freeing yourself from the emotional and energetic ties to a person or situation that led to suffering.[30]

When you Forgive, you not only let go of trying to control or change what has already occurred, but you also release yourself from staying stuck in the past and letting your unresolved hurt bleed into other areas of your life. Forgiveness allows you to be more present in life. In turn, this cultivates more Gratitude. As I mentioned earlier, these acts are intertwined—the more you practice one of them, the more they allow you to experience the other.

If you're finding it hard to Forgive, look at what unresolved pain is lingering.

Is there anger or hurt that you need to express in order to release it? What do you fear would happen if you Forgave? What could you gain by Forgiving? Often, it's those unresolved feelings that lead to you harboring resentment and a need for retribution or justice. By focusing on what's been getting in the way of Forgiveness, you start chipping away at any resistance to create a path to the other side of letting go.

There are two aspects of Forgiveness that are essential to explore: Forgiveness of other and Forgiveness of self. It's natural to focus your attention on external factors that contributed to a change or loss, and blame them for your pain. However, it's important that you also look at what role you may have had in the situation. If you believe you could have done something differently to prevent a change or loss, you'll need to Forgive yourself to move forward.

When I was in my twenties, whenever a romantic relationship ended, I would go through a phase of grief and anger and identify all the things I thought my partner had done wrong. I would do this until I couldn't avoid looking at the other side of the story: the role I had in things ending. This was a painful place for me, because deep down, I already believed that the relationship ending was my fault. I struggled with depression and low self-worth, judging myself harshly and coming up with all kinds of reasons for why someone would leave me: I wasn't pretty enough. I was too controlling. I wasn't carefree and confident. My eyes were brown, not blue. The list went on.

In my 15 years of personal healing work, I learned a reason I got stuck when facing change and loss was because I always blamed myself. I tried to control things by holding more tightly to my pain. Of course, this backfired. Not only was I not allowing myself to move on by refusing to Forgive the other person or myself, I was reinforcing an old story that when things went wrong, it was my fault.

After much work, I learned to see myself with more compassion, and began to Forgive myself for any beliefs of my wrongdoing. I developed greater self-love and confidence, which helped me become more resilient in tough times. I healed, layer by layer, from decades of self-punishment, and I was more able to extend my compassion and Forgiveness toward others and see the opportunities for growth in times of change. I could feel Gratitude for the experience, and Say Goodbye with greater ease.

To begin making room for Forgiveness, ask yourself if you feel ready to change the existing feelings you have toward a hurtful person or situation. If the answer isn't a strong yes, take time to engage in some self-reflection to see what's getting in the way. Practice being present with your emotions–be aware of them without trying to change or avoid their existence–and generate compassion for yourself and others, and the situation.

To Forgive, you have to make a conscious decision to let go of investing your energy in resentment, retribution, or negative emotions that keep you stuck. You take action to release the burden of staying energetically tied to what brought you suffering. How you Forgive is up to you—there isn't a right or wrong way to do it. But one thing I've found very powerful is to engage in a ritual where you set your intention to Forgive and take action to support your intention becoming reality. Below is an example of a ritual that I've used over the years, based on various practices shared by my previous therapists and healers, to assist me with the action of Forgiveness.

To start your Forgiveness ritual, write a letter to the person you were hurt by (or you can write to yourself if self-forgiveness is what you desire). Share the ways you were hurt by that person's (or your own) actions, how they affected you from being able to get closure and move on, and what you desire as you free yourself from the burden of staying stuck. Share what you're grateful for having learned and any wishes you have for that person (or yourself) in the future.

At the end of the letter, you can include a statement of what you want to forgive and release—thoughts, feelings, or behaviors that have held you back from closure—and what new thoughts, feelings, and behaviors you want to put in place. Here's an example:

> I, (insert your name), forgive you, (insert other person's name) for (list the offense). To release us both of any ties to this situation and allow my forgiveness to be complete, here's what I need to say: (share anything that is important for you to say to release feelings of resentment or need for retribution).

After writing your letter, put a match to it, and as it burns, envision yourself being released from any ties to the source of pain. Give thanks for the lessons learned, the ways you grew, and the Gratitude you have for the experience. Then, declare the ritual as complete.

Alternately, you can send the letter to the person, or keep the letter to yourself. I've often found that after I write the letter, the freedom I feel from the past burden is enough and I don't need to send it. Other times, sending the letter has been necessary for me to open a door of communication to try repairing any breaks in a relationship. This is truly a personal choice. Explore both options, and go with the one that feels right for you, ensuring that you surround yourself with the support you need to keep integrating Forgiveness into your life.

If you do send the letter and it opens up a dialogue, you might want to take things a step further by inviting the other person to a conversation facilitated by a professional counselor or therapist. Reaching out for support can be helpful—too often, we isolate ourselves in our pain. An experienced counselor or therapist can act as a neutral party to help you both extend understanding and empathy to each other (and yourselves), as well as establish an action plan for moving forward and healing from the experience.

As you can see, the action of Forgiveness is an interrelated process of being present with your experience, having compassion for it, and learning to let go of what's kept you from getting closure. The more Forgiveness you cultivate, the deeper Acceptance, Understanding, and Gratitude you'll have for your change and loss. Now that you've worked through these four actions, your focus is to integrate what you've learned into a holistic narrative of goodbye. Weaving that narrative into your larger life story will allow you to move forward in carrying out your intention of having a Good Goodbye.

Chapter XII

Saying Goodbye

*"Great is the art of beginning,
but greater is the art of ending."*

—Henry Wadsworth Longfellow

After all this work, you have opened yourself up to fully experience a change or loss, and set a solid foundation to experience a different kind of goodbye. You've learned the importance of self-soothing to manage the stress of change and to cope with the grief of losing an attachment to someone or something you value. You've facilitated greater Acceptance, Understanding, Gratitude, and perhaps Forgiveness for your experience.

With both vulnerability and courage, you are learning to face what scared you about goodbyes in the past and create a new outcome. Now, it's time to integrate all your work up to this point into the final action of Saying Goodbye. This action focuses on you integrating Acceptance, Understanding, Gratitude, and Forgiveness into a holistic story that helps you carry out your intention of having a Good Goodbye experience and feel a sense of completion.

What your Good Goodbye experience will look like depends on what you're Saying Goodbye to: it may involve revisiting a past situation or relationship that ended negatively so you can obtain closure. Or it might involve Saying Goodbye to an existing relationship or current situation that you've struggled to let go. It may be preparing to Say Goodbye to someone or something in the future, or even Saying Goodbye to outdated beliefs that aren't serving your highest good. Whatever the situation, the final action of Saying Goodbye helps you close the chapter on what's changed, honor the grief and the gratitude present in letting go, and Say Goodbye with grace so you can be open and ready for a new chapter to unfold. Let's first discuss what integration means and how it prepares you for the final action of Saying Goodbye.

INTEGRATION

In the field of psychology, self-integration involves having your thoughts, emotions, and actions work in harmony, functioning as a whole. The result is that you become more emotionally connected and trust more in your resilience to get through stressful situations.[31] People who are integrated tend to lead healthier, happier lives than those who aren't as integrated. They have a deep sense of understanding of who they are and how they operate in the world. They are aware of the past stories they have that influence how they perceive new situations. This awareness gives them the capacity to approach situations objectively and not get caught up in feeding stories that don't serve their higher good.[32, 33, 34]

In The Good Goodbye approach, integration means you are connecting to parts of yourself that you couldn't previously access or link together. This includes connecting to any feelings, thoughts, or new insights that came up when going through the previous Good Goodbye actions. When you have unresolved endings or avoid looking at the impact of a change or loss, your experience is fragmented, rather than integrated. For integration to occur, you need to come to a place of objective awareness about yourself and others, and view your experience of change or loss as a whole. In doing so, you let go of attaching to only one part of the experience that keeps you from all the other parts needed to come to closure.

As with the other Good Goodbye actions, integration is a process that requires time and a readiness on your part to view your situation holistically. As you become more integrated, you reframe your goodbye experience by weaving together your recognition of where you've come, where you are now, and where you're heading in a positive way that boosts your self-awareness and, subsequently, your self-esteem. This is how you create a goodbye story that empowers you.

The more aware you are of yourself and integrate that awareness with your experiences moving forward, the more equipped you'll be to create the kind of life you most desire.

When I interviewed Sara, a graduate student in her early thirties, I was struck by the powerful ways she integrated a tragic loss into a story that helped her positively cope with the tragedy. Through deep self-reflection and a commitment to creating a Good Goodbye, Sara transformed what could have been a vicious battle for revenge into a deliberate investment in social justice and personal transformation. Her story, told in the first person, is an inspiration to never lose faith in the power you have within yourself to create healing in the midst of pain.

I was 25 at the time. I was heavily involved in the arts, in a new relationship, and just nothing could go wrong. It was just perfect. Perfect meaning that I was in a place really not thinking about anything specifically that I was trying to work on in my life except for being the next American Idol. That's the path that I was on.

So my father was on the telephone and he was calling to tell me that my brother had been shot. That he was, he was um, dead, and I just needed to get to him. I don't remember exactly what happened next.

Luckily, I had somebody who was very supportive with me at the time. I just remember getting in the car and... that's where my story actually began. Down this road of grieving and dealing with my brother's death. He would have been 15 that month. We were 10 years apart. I helped to raise him.

I remember speaking at his funeral and prior to that, writing down a narrative that I wanted to say during his service. I researched online and found a story that I wanted to model my writing after. [It] was the eulogy for the girls that were in a bombing, I think it might've been in Birmingham, Alabama. And in this eulogy, Dr. Martin Luther King, Jr. had stated something along the lines of, the problem not being the murderer, but the system, the philosophy, and the way of life in that community.

I remember speaking this to my family, my brother's friends, and the community at my brother's funeral. And it was very important that I said these words to them to help us develop a consciousness that this is systemic. And so I'm not sad because there's somebody who murdered my brother, specifically. I needed to do something about what's going on in my neighborhood and make a change. So that was a very powerful moment for me.

I've heard stories before my brother was shot of the statistics about children and youth violence. I never thought it would happen to me and my family. But it happened. And I knew that it was more than just black on black crime or something like that. There's something hidden or underlying, this transcript that was being placed into the community narrative. And it was just a matter of me just uncovering it.

My brother's story and my goodbye story are not just about killing. My brother's death is about life and how to live.

I remember speaking with a newspaper reporter who was interviewing me about what had happened and what I wanted to do about my brother's death. I remember telling him that I just needed to educate myself in order to take the next best step because at that point in my life, I didn't really know how to handle these things. I had gone as far as I could go.

I didn't want there to be conflict between the people and the governmental institutions, like probation departments. The question of how can we work together was important for me. And so in the newspaper article, I said I don't want to be naive, but I think there is a way we can work together.

After that, my father and I started organizing our community by partnering with the foundation Youth UpRising, and others, [like] the Ella Baker Center. We started performing musically at events around the community when there was a death or a family tragedy or something like that.

There was one song in particular called "Stop All Violence on Youth" and we performed that at the California Capitol. After I finished singing, I remember somebody standing up and speaking. I just recall him asking the audience to chant with him, "build California, build." And what he was referring to was more prisons.

So here again was another message. I got a message from writing a piece for my brother's funeral about the philosophies, the way of life, that inspired me to heal our community and then all of a sudden there's this government official who's asking to build prisons. I even had the experience of going to the Oakland City Council and seeing conflict between the people and the council members there. I stopped performing music after that, stopped the performing arts for the most part.

All of these experiences were kind of directing me to continue on with my education because I didn't know how to put all of these pieces of the puzzle together. I knew that in order for me to be able to speak back to people who are in positions of power and who are making decisions out there to build prisons rather than restorative justice programs and things of that nature, I needed to build myself up.

I wanted to understand why humans did the things they did rather than just thinking that they're evil. I knew that there was something more. And so going to college to further my education helped me with all of that.

So that's a snippet, only a snippet of everything that I received from my brother's death that's still continuing to this day. It wasn't a sad goodbye. It was having an understanding of what happened. I was transformed by the goodbye. And although I wish that the story had ended differently, I accepted it. And I knew that for me, it did happen for a reason. So I just needed to think about my own story and what I wanted it to be after that.

I think about the person that actually shot the gun and how that person was impacted, what they may have been experiencing. And I realize that hurt people hurt people. So what am I going to do? Am I going to hurt people back?

In order for me to make it a Good Goodbye, it's not about revenge. Goodbye is being able to have the character to just continue to do good in the world. And also, honestly, from my heart I'm saying it... my brother's goodbye didn't have to be a bad goodbye for that person who shot him either. Because part of the problem is that a lack of understanding and blaming and hatred just perpetuates more of the same.

And so I can only imagine what happened for the person who murdered my brother. And also, I can't just blame that person. I have to look at the larger system of what happened and what needs to change systemically in order to restore justice overall for a community, although I know it's never going to be perfect. The grief is still there, but the way that I deal with it is from a place of understanding.

Recently I was still feeling very sad about things, but when my boyfriend brought me a Dia de los Muertos mask, I actually wore it to work for that day—Dia de los Muertos. It took something away. It took my grief away. I don't know how exactly. It changed something... it made something beautiful,

*not that death is beautiful, but there is... just...
beauty in transformation, that's all.*

*The phrase that really stands out for me is "re-
membering the larger picture." I like to say that in
my brother's death, I found a new life. I have an
understanding, not about the details of why, but a
way of knowing beyond the intellect. In a place
where I would've been broken, I felt whole, even if
there was some mending that was still going on.*

Sara's story describes the powerful experience of feeling
deep grief and transforming it into Gratitude, as losing
her brother led her to peacefully advocate for justice.
This was necessary for her to start integrating the experience of loss into a Good Goodbye—a process that is
ongoing. Though she felt sadness, anger, and defeat, the
desire she had to transform the loss of her brother into
an opportunity to educate herself and create positive action helped her move forward, rather than staying stuck.

When you Accept what life has presented to you and
Understand how you want to move forward—while
choosing to be Grateful for the opportunity to heal and
release yourself from the burden of holding on to any
unfinished business through the act of Forgiveness—you
are integrating your experiences into a story of personal
empowerment. You use your learnings up to this point
to take mastery of your life and how you show up for it
by staying focused on lifting yourself up through the

pain. You connect all your experiences into an updated life story that helps you live in integrity and wholeness. You're not giving in to lollipops of distraction by denying, ignoring, or avoiding yourself and how you operate in life. At this point, you are ready to put everything into the final action of Saying Goodbye.

As you Say Goodbye to what has held you back from healing and closure, you will also replace your old story around goodbyes with a new one. That new story will be informed by all the work you've done in the previous actions of The Good Goodbye approach. Saying Goodbye is a personal process—there isn't one script that will fit every situation. As I shared at the start of this section, you may be Saying Goodbye to a change or loss from the past, facing a current change or loss, or preparing for a change that you're ready to make in the future. That said, there are two steps that can help you in any situation: release and ritual. Let's dive into release first.

RELEASE

It's important to recognize that how things unfold in life isn't all within your control. Goodbyes will happen before you're ready to let go. People involved in your goodbye will make their own decisions and take their own actions. The picture you have of how things should work out will be tested by what life decides to bring you. You can intend to create a Good Goodbye, but you can't always make someone else see the good in your actions, or force them to a place of Acceptance. Life brings you unexpected twists and turns, and you can't control all of it. If you release expectations about how things you *can't* control will unfold, you won't expend unnecessary energy, and can instead focus on what you *can* control, which, in this case, is how you choose to Say Goodbye.

Release is not an abandonment of the work you've done up to this point or a letting go of your responsibility. Rather, it's an acknowledgment that you've done all that you can to take control of how *you* want to show up. Now you can relax into letting what will happen happen. You make room for life to do its part, recognizing that some parts of life are just out of your control.

When you try hard to control because you fear the unknown, you make little room for magic to happen. I think of "magic" as the force of life that's beyond our comprehension. It's the coincidence that happens at the perfect moment to make your wish a reality. It's the inexplicable way that things seem to work out in the end, even when you least expect it. It's what some call God, Spirit, the Universe, fate, or destiny.

While hard science has tended to dismiss this kind of magic, despite it having been an accepted part of many cultures, there's now increasing evidence to empirically demonstrate its validity.[35, 36, 37] For example, scientists are finding that forces such as intuition and unexplained synchronicities (or coincidences) are real and have a significant influence on our lives.[38, 39] Scholars and educators are placing greater importance on the role spirituality plays in authentic, purpose-driven, and joyful lives.[40, 41, 42]

By releasing control and being open to the magic of life, you deepen your trust that whatever happens next is for your higher good. You acknowledge that you may not be able to make the people or circumstances around you do what you want, knowing that you have done your best to lay the groundwork to create the kind of goodbye that most supports what you desire.

Sara's story exemplifies how you can define your desires as you work through a loss, and release control of how others respond. Sara didn't invest in making people right the wrong of her brother's death. Rather, she chose to empower herself through education so she could then use her own voice to advocate for social change. She saw the bigger picture: losing her brother in a tragic way allowed her to learn from it without judgment, and then integrate it into her life story in a positive way.

So how exactly do you Say Goodbye and let go of the outcome when you're investing so much in having things go a certain way? The key is to shift your focus from outward to inward.

Focus less on what you want to happen outside of you and go back to the desired outcome you identified in the action of Understanding.

How do *you* want to get through the experience? Stay invested in those desires; keep them as your focal point as you determine what kind of goodbye you want to say.

One thing that has helped me greatly is to remind myself that I'm not here to make other people learn the lessons that I think they need to learn—even if I think I know best (my sister has reminded me plenty of times of this!). We are each walking our own path, and while we are very much connected on the journey, it's your responsibility to be responsible for you. By taking care to walk in integrity and truth, you can free yourself from trying to control what is out of your control, and at the same time show up accountable and true to yourself as you Say Goodbye.

As you practice releasing expectations of how things should go when you Say Goodbye, continue checking in with yourself about how you feel along the way. Go back to the actions of Acceptance, Understanding, Gratitude, and Forgiveness if you find that you're having a hard time. Then, when you're ready, move forward in carrying out the act of Saying Goodbye.

RITUAL

In my clinical experience as well as my personal journey, I've learned from my instructors, therapists, and healers that one powerful way to Say Goodbye and mark the end of a chapter is to engage in a ritual. Rituals are practiced in every culture—they are symbolic ceremonies undertaken to achieve desires, mark rites of passage, and honor endings.[43, 44, 45] The word *ritual* may bring up images of shamans engaging in a mystical practice, but in fact, you participate in many modern-day rituals all the time.[46] Graduation ceremonies. Retirement parties. Weekly sisterhood gatherings. Your daily morning or bedtime routines. Ritual is a sacred part of our marking our existence through rites of passage, and its magic is accessible to everyone open to incorporating ritual into their lives. In the context of this book, a ritual is a set of symbolic actions you take to celebrate or honor an important moment of change.

We all recognize rites of passage or significant transitional periods such as birthdays, graduations, weddings, promotions, retirement, and death, and we are accustomed to honoring those moments through rituals. But many other moments of transition are ones we don't acknowledge with rituals—think of breakups, job losses, company mergers or closures, or letting go of limiting beliefs and behaviors. Those moments deserve to be honored and celebrated as we would any other rite of passage. Now when I say celebration, I don't mean you're tossing the confetti when your heart's broken. It's not about denying any sadness, anger, or anxiety. Remember, you need to make room for those emotions. But these moments may also bring unexpected feelings like relief, gratitude, or joy, and you must make room for them as well.

As social beings, we're conditioned to behave according to what our society deems acceptable—including how and what we ritualize and celebrate. The same goes for how we Say Goodbye. When we're going through a big change, we automatically reference societal norms as we try to figure out how to think, behave, and feel. Do any of these sound familiar?

"Be strong. Don't cry."

"Keep your voice down."

"Just suck it up and keep moving forward."

"Don't focus on the pain."

"Things could be worse. Look on the brighter side."

By internalizing such common messages, you risk neglecting your needs if they're different from what you're told is acceptable. You indirectly tell yourself that your needs and desires aren't as important as doing what's expected of you. In doing so, it's easy to become less certain of how to get those feelings of security and comfort that you need to cope with the natural stress response to change. As a result, you disconnect further from what you desire—to express all your authentic emotions and positively integrate them into your life.

When you're limited by the norms of what's acceptable to do or not do when Saying Goodbye, you can't explore what will be most healing for *you*. Maybe you need to learn from your ancestors' wisdom in using ritual as sacred ceremony, or create a new ritual that can better honor what you desire. Maybe a long-practiced ritual from your family is what will most help you heal. Whatever the case, give yourself permission to define what ritual means to you, and give yourself lots of room to create the rituals that will most empower you to Say Goodbye with appreciation, celebration, and grace.

I've had personal experience with this. When my grandmother died, I was in her hospital room, and suddenly felt a compelling urge to memorialize her death. Without thinking, I heard myself announce to my family standing over her lifeless body, that it was okay to take photos. Ironically, this was something I had believed was sacrilegious and inappropriate.

Much to my surprise, a line formed. Each relative handed me their phone, eager to have me take a picture. "Here, *mi hijita*, can you please take a picture of me with my mother?" "Cousin, I want you to take a picture of me kissing my *Abuelita*." "*Gracias, mi amor,* I am going to keep this picture forever."

That day, I captured pictures that would be cherished for a lifetime, pictures that portrayed my family members experiencing the transformational rite of passage of death. These images would serve to remind my relatives that they didn't have to be restricted by previous beliefs of what they should do or how they should act when facing a change or loss. Taking these photos gave them permission to Say Goodbye to my grandmother the way they desired. Had we not made a ritual of it, a few people may have snuck in their photos, but the rest of them would have missed the opportunity to feel they had the power to do so out of fear that such a behavior was unacceptable and inappropriate.

By implementing a ritual as a way to Say Goodbye, you symbolically honor the transition from one moment in life to another, and manifest your desire to become transformed through the process.

In order to be fully open to this transformation, you have to release control of how it will occur. This is where you need to honor what you're losing and embrace what has yet to come as you transition, recognizing that you can't control everything, but you can control how you show up for it. Ritual becomes the galvanizing force to propel you forward in trusting your experiences and allowing things to unfold as you cross over to a new chapter.[47, 48]

Goodbyes are commonly ritualized when we're children—think of how your elementary school teacher prepared you and your classmates to say goodbye at the end of a school year, or how your parents ritualized losing a tooth that would be picked up in the night by the Tooth Fairy. But as we get older, we often miss chances to Say Goodbye through ritualizing important moments of transition. Take work transitions, for example. How many times have you experienced or heard of a layoff that involved employees being called in for a sudden meeting, told they no longer have a job, walked to their desk to collect their personal belongings, and then escorted directly out of the building? Where's the chance to Say Goodbye? To digest what's happening? To have a voice in the matter? It often doesn't exist, because companies want to minimize the risk of retaliatory behavior.

There are more examples: Experiencing a breakup via text or email. Being stood up on a date. Friendships fading away over time. Being unfriended on social media. We learn to avoid dealing with the uncomfortable but necessary part of letting go by just vanishing and hoping the other person won't care or notice. We don't recalibrate our stress to get to a place of feeling comforted and secure. We don't honor the transition through any kind of ritual. The impact of these kinds of goodbyes—in which there is little to no acknowledgment and certainly no honoring of the transition—can be devastating.

Instead, you can choose to Say Goodbye to these kinds of situations and others by seeing them as rites of passage and opportunities for personal growth and transformation. You can design your own rituals to memorialize change and loss so they can be infused with the feelings you desire. You can let go of any societal expectations of what you should and shouldn't do, and instead choose to act in a way that will most help you obtain closure.

Let me give you some examples of rituals I've used in my own goodbyes. In my work as a psychotherapist, I learned the importance of ritualizing the end of a therapeutic relationship to help my clients experience a healthy goodbye. Several weeks before our professional relationship ended, I would begin preparing my client (and me) for our upcoming goodbye. We would spend the subsequent weeks reviewing the client's progress and successes and what lessons they were carrying forward. We would talk about how the client wanted to spend their last session with me and then on the final day, we would carry out that wish. We would talk about any sadness or grief they were feeling and express our mutual gratitude for the bond we had created. We would exchange small tokens of appreciation to mark the end of our relationship. Then, we would say good-bye.

For many clients who had gone through negative, complicated endings such as divorces or the sudden death of loved ones, this was the first time they experienced ritualizing an ending that was positive. This experience gave them a template for how they could say goodbye differently in the future.

Another example of ritualizing a goodbye came when I was preparing to close NHU. I had a small team of employees who would work with me through the last day before we closed our doors. Months before, I asked my team how they wanted to say goodbye on the last day. They developed a proposal of options that wholeheartedly reflected what they needed and desired to feel a sense of completion—they wanted room to be sad and to celebrate all the hard work that went into closing down operations. They wanted to leave some sort of legacy behind, a symbol or object that reminded people that NHU once existed on the property. They didn't want to be alone after driving out of the parking lot. Finally, they wanted to be able to relax now that things were done.

In the following weeks, I helped ritualize those desires to support the employees Saying Goodbye. In our Daily Dip meetings, we talked about how we were feeling getting closer to our last day. We supported the university community in honoring the university closure through hosting an amazingly powerful and heartfelt final commencement ceremony. We installed plaques on benches that told the story of NHU.

On our final day, we invited members of the university community to join our team in saying our final goodbye to the university. A healer blessed the gathering and our wishes for our grief to transform into appreciation and joy. Our team had a symbolic moment of embrace as we took a final look at our space and then closed the door. A mariachi band played as we walked out of the building, filling our hearts with celebration and light. When we were outside the building, I handed an invitation to my team to meet me at a surprise destination where we would not only relax and celebrate all our hard work, but honor each employee's incredible contributions to upholding our vision of creating a Good Goodbye.

If you're new to ritual, I invite you not to get caught up in thinking you have to create something complicated. While ritual is a very sacred practice that does require clear, pure intention and purpose, it can also be a space to be creative in shaping something that most speaks to your heart. In the case of NHU, our goodbye ritual sprang from the wishes and desires my team expressed to me. From there, I was able to give my team what they needed to Say Goodbye.

While creating a ritual does take intention and planning, you can also incorporate it in situations of sudden loss and fresh grief. Take the case of my neighbor, Ana.

One morning, I was drinking tea and responding to emails when Ana stopped by. Crying, she shared that she'd just found out her cat, Black, had a large tumor in his lungs that was restricting his breathing. The vet said he would have to be put down that very day. Imagine the stress and shock of learning that a loved one is not only sick, but will have their life end in a matter of hours.

As Ana shared the details, I asked her some questions to deal with my own difficulty hearing the news. She clearly stated that Black's life was quickly coming to a close. She knew she had to Accept what she was facing. I asked what options she had to Say Goodbye to Black how she desired. Could she spend more time with him at home? Did she have to see him take his final breath at the veterinarian clinic? Ana wasn't sure, but knew there were more questions she needed answered to help her continue adjusting to the sudden news.

Ana was in shock and grief. Yet, I observed this beautiful strength she had to identify the opportunity in front of her: she could choose how she wanted to Say Goodbye to Black. She could make it a Good Goodbye. Ana shared how she wanted to be present for what was happening and not avoid showing up fully for these last moments with Black. She expressed Gratitude for the six-year relationship she had with him, as well as the opportunity she had to be with him as he passed, rather than finding him dead one day.

I encouraged Ana to determine what a Good Goodbye would look like for her. She said she wanted to be with him at home where he could be surrounded by a familiar comfort. So, in a series of visits to the clinic where she continued to consult with her vet, she was able to arrange for Black to return home so she could be with him in his final moments. In taking care to plan out her goodbye with the intention of making it a loving, positive experience for her and Black, Ana was ritualizing this rite of passage of death. She arranged their last night together to be one of peace, calm, and love. She set up a small altar in honor of him and placed his collar and a clipping of his hair on it. By his side in his final moment, she Said Goodbye.

What struck me deeply about Ana's loss was her ability to see the blessings available to her in the freshness of grief: she got to be with Black before he passed, practice being present with her pain, and cherish those last moments with clarity and purpose. For years, Ana had maintained a daily practice of gratitude and self-reflection. Now, she could lean on her practice to get her through the stress of this loss. Her ability to do this within hours of being hit with the shocking news was incredible. It reinforced my conviction that:

When you Accept what's in front of you, you free yourself up to move through a change or loss with more ease.

And when you take intentional action to symbolically Say Goodbye through a ritual, you can infuse that moment with the blessings of love, surrender, and grace.

In my personal work with therapists and healers, I've learned that Saying Goodbye through ritual can be as simple as writing a goodbye letter to a loved one; lighting a candle and sending your hopes and fears to the flame; taking three minutes of meditation to send your wishes for healing for yourself and others; preparing a sacred bath to cleanse your soul. Rituals help you practice Gratitude for the lessons being brought to you, release control to the larger force of life that will determine what unfolds next, and trust your capacity to get through it in the way you most desire.

When you engage in a ritual, it's important to end it with closing words and actions. This involves acknowledging the purpose of your ritual, expressing appreciation for it, and intentionally marking the ritual as complete. This also helps release you and anyone else involved in the ritual from carrying forward any "unfinished business," and symbolizes your intent to surrender to the unfolding of a new chapter, one in which you've clearly set your intention for what you desire and allow the larger forces in life to play their part in making those desires reality.

When you reach the point of being ready and willing to Say Goodbye, acknowledge that moment with a ritual of your design. Use the ritual to symbolically release your attachment to an old goodbye story that kept you stuck, anyone or anything you're saying goodbye to, and to a chapter closing. Know that whenever you go through another significant change or loss, you can invoke that ritual to both honor what's ending and also to celebrate a new beginning. You can also create different rituals to honor different types of situations. The intentionality you place in shaping how you Say Goodbye will infuse your efforts with energy to uphold the good throughout each experience.

To help you begin incorporating rituals into Saying Goodbye, I strongly recommend you start by taking note of the kinds of rituals you've already participated in with your family, loved ones, or other communities you're a part of. Think about what made those rituals significant. Were there certain prayers, symbolic actions, or certain objects that were used? Identify what elements of past rituals you feel closely connected to and try incorporating them into your own ritual when you want to symbolically honor a change. Talk to others about how they've used rituals in their own lives to generate new ideas.

Reach out to trusted healers, elders, and other mentors who can guide you on how to use ritual in ways that honor your clear intentions. You'll also find additional ideas and examples in the last part of the book.

SAYING THE GOODBYE

Now that you've gotten this far in preparing to Say Goodbye, what comes next? If you haven't already Said Goodbye through a ritual, now is the time to say it. What does that look like? What will happen when you do it? Will things go as you hoped? Remember, you've done so much work to identify your desires for how you want to get through this experience, and compassionately prepared yourself to let go with grace. It's now time to carry out your desires so they manifest into reality.

As we discussed earlier, how you Say Goodbye is unique to the experience you're facing. If you're struggling to know how to carry out the act, spend some time reflecting on your ideal outcome. For example, if you're Saying Goodbye to a current relationship that you're ready to end, or to someone with whom things didn't end well in the past, write out a script of what you want to say to that person. If you're struggling to know what to say, talk to someone you trust to generate some ideas. Stay focused on controlling what you can and let go of what you can't. Surround yourself with support and take care to self-soothe as you deal with any stress that comes up. Reflect on The Good Goodbye actions you've taken up until now, and then go forth and Say Goodbye, knowing you are ready to face whatever unfolds.

After you Say Goodbye, you can use the same Good Goodbye actions of Acceptance, Understanding, Gratitude, and Forgiveness to assess and work through having said the goodbye. Start by Accepting what happened without trying to change it. Recognize and review what unfolded with as little judgement or insertion of what you think should have happened.

Next, Understand how you feel having Said Goodbye, and determine how you want to feel as you integrate what happened into your new goodbye story. Did someone respond the way you had hoped? Did you show up the way you desired? Did you reach the outcome you were looking for?

Allow yourself to work through any emotions that come up so you don't get stuck on one end of the emotional spectrum. Maybe you're sad that you actually Said Goodbye. Or someone else's reaction to the goodbye hurt your feelings. Alternately, you might feel tremendous relief, like a weight has been lifted from your shoulders. Use the exercises in *The Good Goodbye Blueprint* and questions in the Understanding section of the book to sift through where you are and determine where you want to be now that the goodbye is behind you.

To foster Gratitude for the experience, identify what lessons, healing, and new openings emerged in the process.

What did you gain by Saying Goodbye? What are you thankful for in seeing how things unfolded?

Work to Forgive yourself and anyone involved for any hurt or resentment that may have come up from Saying Goodbye. Stay present with your experience, cultivate compassion for yourself and others, and continue taking care to self-soothe and manage any stress that comes up.

Lastly, integrate your experience by creating a holistic narrative about what happened so you honor the good along with the hurt, if any remains. Reinforce this new Good Goodbye story by continually practicing Gratitude for the experience, honoring the lessons learned as you update any thoughts, emotions, or behaviors that were holding you back, and allowing yourself to revisit how you're doing along the way. Honor having gone through the action of Saying Goodbye through a practice of Gratitude (an example is included in *The Good Goodbye Blueprint*).

As I mentioned early on, going through the actions of The Good Goodbye approach does not guarantee that everything is healed and solved forever; there will be ongoing work. The process of updating your goodbye story and staying open to finding the good in times of change is a lifelong commitment. The more you practice applying it, the greater ease you'll have incorporating it in challenging times.

So what happens if you go through all the actions, engage in a ritual and truly feel like you are releasing expectations and control, but then a few days later you still feel that there's unfinished business? Or new emotions come up that you weren't expecting?

A yoga instructor of mine shared a quote that, in essence, said: "When you experience a breakdown, there will inevitably be a breakthrough to reaching your full potential." The inverse is also true. When you have a breakthrough, which in this case can be getting unstuck from your old goodbye story and feeling the momentum of stepping forward more unburdened, you can subsequently experience a breakdown.

This could be you uncovering another layer of grief that you haven't worked through, or could feel like a strong pull to not move forward after Saying Goodbye. If this happens, let it be what it is without trying to change it. Accept any thoughts or emotions that rise up and try to Understand them with compassion and without judgment. Practice Gratitude for what's come up. Once again, you're engaging in the actions of The Good Goodbye approach; they can get you through any new resistance or difficulty.

Your life is an interconnected web of experiences, so when you revisit one experience that you previously avoided or had a hard time dealing with, it can trigger other points in the web that also need your attention.

Maybe you're not quite ready to Forgive. Or in doing a ritual of release, you suddenly feel nostalgic and don't want to let someone go. Unexpected thoughts and emotions arise, and you might feel like they're setting you back. It's natural to have these responses. Look at them as another opportunity to sift through the many layers of loss that surround an experience. Be realistic, patient, and gentle with yourself; don't expect that everything will be healed once you've gone through The Good Goodbye approach one time.

If in going through the actions again you still feel stuck, enroll the support of others, in particular a professional counselor, therapist, or healer. There may be some deeper work that needs to happen for you to release any early experiences in life that got put away until now. You will want to have the guidance and support of someone trained to deal with any complicated grief or unresolved loss so you don't continue struggling trying to figure things out on your own.

And remember, The Good Goodbye approach is not something that stops once you Say Goodbye. Now that you've begun a new chapter, the work ahead of you is to integrate the experience you had in a way that continues to uplift you as you go through life. The next time a change happens, you can face it and practice the actions of The Good Goodbye approach to create a new goodbye story for that particular experience. Each time, you'll discover new lessons, uncover old stories and beliefs that have held you back, and get a new chance to heal what you're ready to let go of. Let The Good Goodbye be a way of living that helps you navigate life's changes with more ease.

To help you explore how to create your own Good Goodbye, the next part of the book offers stories of people going through different types of change, and shows how they tailored The Good Goodbye actions to their unique situations. I hope these stories give you inspiration to keep staying the course. Additionally, as you complete *The Good Goodbye Blueprint* exercises, you'll generate new ideas to implement a Good Goodbye. As always, if you find you're stuck or having a hard time, reach out for help and be open to receiving it. It's hard enough going through change. Don't make it harder by struggling through it alone.

III.

CREATING
GOOD
GOODBYES

"

If you're brave enough to say goodbye,
life will reward you with a new hello.

— Paulo Coelho

Chapter XIII

Knowing When it's Time to Say Goodbye

"How lucky am I to have something that makes saying goodbye so hard."

- Winnie the Pooh

In the past, you've seen the ways you suffer when you hold on to outdated beliefs or goodbye stories, focus only on what you've lost, and ignore the blessings you've gained. Now you realize it's time to Accept what's in front of you and allow yourself to move on. It can be scary to do this, and if others are involved, there is the added stress of dealing with their potential feelings or reactions. But you know that if you don't take action, you'll only end up prolonging your suffering—and at this point, that's no longer an option.

This is what happened for J.T. with his friend, Eva. She kept dragging them through the past breach of trust and it was taking a toll on their friendship. J.T. was able to develop more compassion and understanding of her struggle, but in the end he concluded that things would not change much, even with time, and that the friendship was affecting his quality of life. After our work together, J.T. ultimately made the decision to Say Goodbye to the relationship.

J.T. could Accept that his friendship had deteriorated over the years and he was stuck. He stopped placing blame—either on himself or Eva—for what had happened, and simply acknowledged the situation for what it was.

To establish the action of Understanding, I took J.T. through some exercises to help him identify his existing experience and desired outcome. His existing experience involved feeling unhappiness, frustration, and discouragement in his friendship. He wanted to feel thankful, hopeful, and reinvested in establishing better boundaries in all his friendships. We explored what had been preventing him from achieving his desired outcome. Trust issues, guilt, lack of self-compassion, and unhealed past wounds of broken trust came up. J.T. recalled the betrayals he'd experienced throughout life, but also remembered Eva had similar experiences in her history. This gave him more compassion for her, recognizing that they were both suffering through current issues in their friendship as well as old hurts from the past.

Next, J.T.'s work was to use the action of Gratitude to weave his new perspectives into a story that allowed him to move forward with appreciation, hope, and a renewed sense of investment in creating healthier boundaries. His compassion for his and Eva's experiences motivated him to revisit how he abruptly cut her out of his life. He had some difficulty moving through the action of Forgiveness—forgiving himself and how he treated Eva out of anger, and forgiving Eva for the ways she wouldn't let him move on from the betrayal of trust. But he was eventually able to work through it by creating a ritual.

In addition to working through Forgiveness, J.T. also needed to let go of lingering resentment and release expectations and outcome—part of the action of Saying a Good Goodbye. We decided a ritual might help him do all these things, and together, we identified what that ritual would look like. He wanted it to include the support of loved ones, self-care, and some objects that symbolized cleansing and letting go. That evening, he spent quality time with his sister. He then took a rejuvenating, cleansing bath where he lit a candle with the wish to stay in a space of appreciation and compassion for himself and Eva. He gave himself time in solitude to reflect on his wishes for the friendship. With resolve to reconnect with Eva with more compassion and honesty, he released his past grip on anger and resentment. He freed himself of any desire to control her response, and found himself open to whatever reaction she would have to him choosing to let their friendship go.

J.T. then moved on to the action of Saying a Good Goodbye. He reached out to Eva, with the aim of having an open, mature conversation about their inability to get on the same page. During the conversation, she acknowledged and agreed that their bond had been worn thin and things just didn't feel the same anymore. After talking things through, they agreed to respectfully let the friendship end without any harbored resentment. Each person was able to move forward with clarity as to why the relationship ended; this was a significant leap from where J.T. began, when he abruptly cut off ties with Eva without explanation.

The clarity J.T. and Eva felt about why they were ending their friendship was a great gift for both of them. This clarity is a gift I want you to experience in your own endings. It may feel easiest to just let things fade away, make excuses each time you get invited to spend time with someone you'd rather not invest your energy in, or try sweeping things under the rug. You may not want to be seen as the "bad guy," or you may fear judgment or rejection. However, all this does is complicate matters, because avoidance doesn't mean the issues have vanished. They remain there unaddressed, and they limit your chance to learn and grow from the experience. You have the choice to end what's not working in your life; you must also take responsibility for it.

Honestly acknowledging your need to create an end can be a gift for you and anyone else involved.

You're creating an opportunity to release each other of needing to hold on to anything out of misunderstanding or confusion. You create the conditions for a Good Goodbye. However, it does not guarantee how the other person will respond. Despite your best efforts, you cannot control another person's actions. You are only responsible for yourself.

What would have happened if Eva didn't respond so openly to ending the friendship? What if she had responded with anger, denial or despair? Would it mean all of J.T.'s work to create the conditions for a Good Goodbye would be lost? No. J.T. would still have the opportunity to make it a positive experience for himself. Remember, Saying Goodbye is less about what the other person does and more about how it helps *you* close a chapter feeling empowered to move forward.

If someone doesn't respond the way you want when you're Saying Goodbye, practice going through The Good Goodbye actions to let go of negatively attaching to their response. Let's look at how that might have unfolded in J.T.'s story.

Imagine that Eva gets angry in hearing that J.T. wants to end the friendship, and in her grief, she starts blaming J.T. for things not working out. Instead of retaliating, J.T. knows he must focus on 1) taking care of himself in response to her outburst and 2) taking care to uphold his desire to have a Good Goodbye.

First, J.T. can Accept Eva's negative response without judgment. He may even say to Eva, "I see that you're angry and I want to make room for that, as I get this must be hard for you to hear."

Next, he can work to Understand and appreciate her reaction with compassion and empathy, as he also takes care to self-soothe and reflect on how her response affects him. J.T. can invite Eva to help him understand why she's angry. He can listen to what she has to say and practice not reacting to it with his own anger or resentment. If J.T. feels her anger is unsafe for him, he can choose to remove himself from the situation. In both scenarios, J.T. stays focused on compassionately recognizing what he's facing and moving toward his vision of a Good Goodbye.

If in listening to Eva talk about her anger, J.T. feels safe to stay engaged with her, he can thank her for sharing her feelings and express what he's thankful for in having been friends for eight years. Telling Eva, "I'm thankful for you and what you brought to my life" can be soothing to her; remember, she's also struggling to find her own ways to self-soothe and cope with the stress of losing the friendship. J.T. can also reiterate his decision to end the friendship and his hope that they can do so together through some sort of ritual that helps them Say Goodbye.

If J.T. doesn't feel it's safe to continue the conversation with Eva in person, he can still carry out saying a Good Goodbye on his own by writing her a letter expressing the same desires mentioned above, and do one of three things with it: 1) He can burn the letter as a ritual of release; 2) He can send the letter to her without expecting a response back; 3) He can not send the letter and offer a wish that both he and Eva find their own ways to closure with grace and compassion.

If you allow yourself to create a goodbye that honors everyone involved, upholds the values that are most essential for you to live with integrity, and gives you a chance to evolve into a new space that better suits your needs, you can find that creating closure isn't something to be feared. Rather, it can be a sacred opportunity to embrace what's come to an end, knowing that it will lead you to deeper healing and a greater ability to fully move on. Let's look at The Good Goodbye approach as it's applied to some other common endings you may experience.

Chapter XIV

Saying Goodbye to Outdated Beliefs

"In the end, these things matter most:
How well did you love? How fully did you live?
How deeply did you let go?"

- Jack Kornfield

Sometimes, a belief or value you've had throughout life starts to require too much energy to maintain. Because we invest so much in the stories we tell ourselves about who we are and how our world works, it's hard to gain perspective to accurately assess which beliefs could use an update or even a retirement. In addition, many of us simply move through life on automatic pilot, without experiencing true self-awareness or even a sense of what thoughts and values drive our actions.

However, taking the time to look inward is extremely valuable, and can illuminate areas of your life that are thriving and, conversely, areas where you're stuck. You can then dive into those stuck areas to see what beliefs need some cleaning up, and let the really outdated versions go through a Good Goodbye.

After my mom died in 2003, I began to dread the holidays. I responded to any signs of Christmas that came up after Halloween with a "bah-humbug" attitude that would have made Ebenezer Scrooge proud. It felt wrong to me to celebrate a time of year while also grieving my mom's passing; as a result, my beliefs about the holidays changed from jolly cheer to unhappy disenchantment. What I didn't realize was that I was reinforcing a lack of appreciation during the Christmas season, a period that had always been a time of celebration for me.

On a recent Christmas Day, I decided to face these beliefs. I had come to the point of recognizing that they were holding me back from feeling happiness and were keeping me stuck in grief.

I remembered that for my family, Christmas always brought mixed emotions. For much of my childhood, the days before Christmas were filled with anticipation of Santa's arrival and excitement about the gifts that would soon fill the space underneath the Christmas tree. But the holidays also held moments of disappointment and sadness.

In my Mexican-Peruvian household, Latin music would intermingle with traditional American holiday tunes as extended family members would come over to spend Christmas Eve with my family. At the stroke of midnight, chocolaté and pannetone—homemade Mexican hot chocolate and a sweet bread similar to fruitcake—would be passed around, and gifts exchanged. I remember watching as each person opened gifts and wondering when I would receive mine. I paid attention to the number of gifts each person received, and felt a pang in my heart for those who just received one. In my mind, more gifts meant more love.

Though the gifts clearly consumed a lot of my energy, I was also aware of the accumulated pressure that accompanied the holidays—pressure to have the money to buy the gifts, cook all the food, and have a peaceful holiday— and how it seemed to get the best of my parents. There was enough stress in our household with my mom working three jobs, my dad frustrated and worried about her working too much, and both of them struggling to maintain a steady income to pay the bills. If Christmas could just be a time of joy and peace, it would ease the challenges we dealt with the rest of the year.... or so I wanted to believe.

My mom would get angry that the meaning of Christmas was lost as the focus on gifts and materialism took center stage. She'd get so stressed trying to sell enough cakes in her cake business to have the money to buy all the gifts she felt obligated to get for the 50 (yep, that's not a typo) first cousins I had who were new to America and to the concept of gifts. My father would get angry seeing my mom under so much stress, and naturally, this led to friction between them that colored the overall mood of the holiday.

On a few occasions, after my parents went to bed, I would sneak to the Christmas tree and cry. I cried for not having a peaceful Christmas. I cried that my parents were fighting. I cried that my dream and wish for a happy holiday to offset the stress that was present the rest of the year didn't seem to be coming true.

Each year that passed, the same tension hung in the air, and I became less sure that Christmas could ever be what I desired. But I wasn't ready to let go of the dream. I tried to fix things by buying gifts... lots of them. I thought that if others could feel the love that I felt with each gift they opened, and if there were many gifts to go around, then there would be lots of love and happiness in my family, and my wish would come true. But it didn't work. I didn't realize that by doing this, I was actually adopting some of the stress I'd observed in my parents. Over time, Christmases left me feeling defeated and sorrowful. I beat myself up for caring so much about these damn gifts and continuing to desire that happy family experience. Finally, I stopped trying as much. I began doubting. My hope dwindled. My wish was fading. Then, my mom died.

For several years after my mom's death, I responded with anger to all things Christmas. I would become furious at the first sighting of a Christmas tree. I would wince at the sounds of holiday cheer. The day before

Christmas, I would finally muster the energy to hurriedly buy gifts for my loved ones, replacing the beautifully wrapped packages of the past with simple gift bags. I had stopped caring. I stopped believing that dream could be fulfilled. The happy family that celebrated Christmas without fights and opened up gifts at midnight in loving celebration of the season of thanks... it could never happen with my mom gone.

Seven years after my mom's passing, my sister and her husband proposed a new idea for Christmas: no gifts. Instead of freeing me from the angst of the past, the proposal sent me into an unexpected tailspin. "We can't *not* have gifts! Gifts are part of what Christmas is about!" I cried. My sister responded as compassionately as she could, pointing out that gifts have nothing to do with Christmas, that I was the one that had put so much meaning into them, and it was time to let that go.

Her words finally broke through to me, and I began to undertake the action of Acceptance. I Accepted that my past beliefs about what Christmas meant and the story I created that I could never have a happy Christmas without my mom were keeping me stuck. They were not helping me acknowledge that I could still create new experiences of joy without her.

I reflected on my situation and recognized how my current feelings of resentment toward holiday cheer, sadness about my mom having died, and anger at not having a past dream fulfilled no longer served me. I desired more love, joy, and fun. I was now working through the second action of Understanding. What held me back in the past from getting the love, joy, and fun I desired— the gap in between where I currently was and where I wanted to be— was grief, guilt of moving on without my mom, and resistance to forgiving myself for acting in ways that I judged as angry or bah-humbug-y.

To integrate my desires into a new story that would help me be open to new experiences, I worked with my sister to find a compromise on gifts. We decided to start a new tradition—a white elephant gift exchange. Each person buys just one gift. Everyone draws numbers, and we all go in order to choose gifts. Gifts can be taken, retrieved, and retaken, and finally, everyone ends up with one gift that they call their own.

The first year we did the white elephant gift exchange, I remember watching laughter and lightness fill the room. The gifts were all expressions of love and playfulness, and the game brought holiday cheer to our home. I was developing Gratitude for the new experience—and this was only possible because I had Accepted that it was time to let go of an old dream. My desires were indeed becoming my new reality. The old belief that more gifts meant more love and could overcome the fighting, pressure, and disappointment of the holidays was replaced with new experiences of joy. There was still hope that Christmas could be a time of happiness for my family.

For four years now, my family has implemented this Christmas gift exchange and every single time, the same results happen. It's been beautiful.

> **Rather than continuing to force the love and happiness I desired to happen, my family and I were able to Say Goodbye to traditions of the past.**

In doing so, we made room for all sorts of new possibilities, including ones that could bring about the exact thing I'd been longing for my entire life.

I decided it was time to honor my letting go of those old beliefs and dreams. I was ready to move on to Forgiveness of myself for being stuck in resentment and anger, and Forgive my family for not having the easiest time getting through not just the holidays, but life in general.

I woke up one Christmas morning, knelt down next to the Christmas tree, and through tears of Gratitude, gave thanks to my mom, my dad, my sister, and myself for our life together as a family. I gave thanks for the many blessings I received in my mom's passing. I gave myself a lot of compassion for the ways in which I struggled to let go. I celebrated the new experiences I was having with our white elephant tradition. I set an intention to become more open to celebrating the joy of Christmas. Finally, I Said Goodbye to it all by journaling my experiences, ritualistically lighting a candle, and then symbolically letting it all go.

Updating your beliefs allows for new life experiences. This is part of the process of change. As you evolve, what you desire also evolves. Rather than ignore the expiration of old desires and dreams, acknowledge their transformation. Recognize that you're letting them go to invite the realization of new dreams into your life. Honor the role they served up until this point in time and, through your own ritual, release them through a Good Goodbye.

Chapter XV

Saying Goodbye at Work

"In our lives, change is unavoidable, loss is unavoidable. In the adaptability and ease with which we experience change lies our happiness and freedom."

- Buddha

I remember the first time I was laid off at work. Within the space of an hour, I received the shocking news, was escorted to my desk, and then shown the door, without a chance to say goodbye to my colleagues. I drove away in shame; it was a terribly humiliating experience.

Sadly, this layoff experience is a common one. Unfortunately, in rushing the goodbye process to minimize risk of retaliation or emotional outbursts, companies ensure the experience becomes traumatic. A similar thing often happens with company mergers, acquisitions, or closures. I live in San Francisco, just north of Silicon Valley, where company startups happen as quickly as they shut down. I can't tell you how many stories I've heard of employees not feeling there's space to grieve a change in the organization, let alone celebrate it if the change is one that can move the company in a positive direction.

When organizational change is on the horizon, employees often go about their business as if nothing huge is happening, quietly speculating on what departments or positions will be eliminated when the other company takes over. Think back to Renee's story (page 44). If there is any communication from management, it's often in the form of carefully-worded emails that focus on the benefits of the change. This communication is important, but what's equally important—and almost never happens—is making space for employees to grieve. To share their fear and disappointment. To be trusted to have human experiences that won't lead to more chaos. To be supported and empowered so they can manage the natural stress that comes with such change.

It's understandable that going through a significant organizational change and the related emotions can be daunting. So we often try to avoid, minimize, or downplay the change and the feelings. This applies whether you're the CEO of a Fortune 100 company or an employee of a small business. We all have our own process of dealing with goodbyes, and when they come up at work, our own personal stories of goodbyes, compounded with our culture's fear of change and difficulty embracing endings, influence the decisions we make. And if we avoid facing goodbyes out of fear, everyone suffers.

However, there is another way to manage organizational transitions such as employee layoffs or resignations and company mergers, restructuring, or closures: create an environment that embraces change and the opportunity it brings for transformation and healing. We have to start by changing how we view goodbyes, and trust ourselves and others enough to let go of our old stories and embark on a new experience that focuses on the good in letting go.

Even if you're not in charge of your company to influence how change is managed, you can still take charge of how you work through the change. Veronica's story is a good example of this. Veronica was able to use The Good Goodbye approach to further heal from the separation from her abusive relationship. She also applied the approach to another change she was facing.

Some time after our interview, I got a surprising email from her. She had applied The Good Goodbye approach to her job situation and decided it was time to resign. How she chose to do so demonstrates a new way to honor endings at work that can be an empowering experience for everyone involved.

Veronica was very happy at her job, but after breaking up with her boyfriend, she continued to live in the same small town because it was near her workplace. It was hard for her to meet new friends, and she felt stuck there, but the thought of making a move after the breakup felt overwhelming. However, after our interview, she started to reassess her life situation.

Veronica Accepted that she felt stuck where she was living and didn't feel like she was fully moving on from her ex by staying in the town where their relationship had unfolded. She went through the action of Understanding to assess where she was and where she wanted to be. She currently felt unhappy, isolated, and uninspired. She felt like she was just going through the motions each day, keeping up the same routine without much enthusiasm. She wanted to feel excited by meeting new people, energized by her surroundings, and open to a new chapter where a new living environment could be part of the picture. She now knew she deserved to be happy in life and put herself first, something she learned from her breakup.

When Veronica looked at the gap between where she was and wanted to be by identifying what kept her from her desires, she saw that her guilt at the prospect of leaving her job and letting her colleagues down was holding her back. She knew that to keep the healing she had done going, she needed to be open to letting that guilt go and make more room for what she truly wanted. She fostered Gratitude by appreciating all she had learned at her job, reminding herself that she wasn't a bad person for wanting to move on to a new chapter, and that in starting something new, she was continuing to reinforce that her utmost happiness was a priority.

Veronica had made her decision—she was going to move to a new town. She knew this meant leaving her job and facing her fear of letting people down. In the past, Veronica had followed the standard two weeks' notice when leaving jobs. However, this time was different. She shared with me that as much as she wanted to avoid telling people at work that she would be quitting, she didn't want to recreate the experience of waiting until the last minute to give notice. She wanted to make her transition a Good Goodbye.

She didn't know what would happen if she told her boss that she was going to start looking for a new job. Her fear was that she would be fired. But by releasing expectations or attempts to try to control the outcome and still follow through with Saying a Good Goodbye, she decided to tell her boss that she was planning on moving in several months.

Her boss was surprised. In fact, Veronica was the first employee at that organization to give more than two weeks' notice and offer ample time to help work out her transition. Her colleagues expressed their appreciation for the chance to thoughtfully plan their farewells. On her last day at work, Veronica ritualized her experience by creating a Good Goodbye celebration with her colleagues. This allowed everyone involved to close a chapter with a shared sense of Acceptance, Understanding, Gratitude, and celebration.

Work goodbyes don't have to ignore the human experience of grief and loss.

If you're affected by a layoff or other workplace change, or see that colleagues are, share your emotions or invite coworkers to share theirs. Encourage them to join you for a Good Goodbye sendoff. Don't keep up the status quo of pretending nothing's happening because you're afraid. Recognize that you have a lot of power to help yourself and others experience endings in a new way that can bring healing.

And if you're in a leadership position, strive to influence your organization's culture so it provides room for grief and celebration. Work to redefine how organizational transitions are managed so they're more inclusive of the heart of your organization: the employees. As Veronica's story showed, you'll likely get a positive, appreciative response from those around you.

Chapter XVI

Saying Goodbye to Relationships

"This is a good sign, having a broken heart.
It means we have tried for something."

– Elizabeth Gilbert

Remember your first "real" relationship breakup? You know, the one that left you crawling into your bed, not showering or brushing your teeth for days, and only leaving your bedroom to take a nibble out of that box of long-expired Lucky Charms stuffed in the back of your kitchen cupboard. Ah, yes...that one. So what happened?

You got over it. You moved on. You may have even mended things with your ex and now have a great friendship in place. Those breakups—where you part with a strong understanding about why things ended, thankful for the lessons learned and clear about what you want in your next relationship—make you stronger. But perhaps more often, breakups are not-so-great endings that leave a residue of unfinished business in your heart.

Whether you're dealing with a romantic relationship, a marriage, or a friendship, how you choose to end things affects how you'll cope and move on. Some relationships end with fireworks and grand gestures of heartache. Others fizzle out over time, with a slowly-growing emotional distance that results in ultimate separation. In each instance, the signs are there, telling you it's time to close the chapter. But often there's a thread of hope that keeps you holding on, sometimes way past the expiration date. How often have you stayed in a relationship gone sour because you were afraid to end it?

Being aware of and able to Accept what's showing up in a relationship requires openness to self-reflection. Often, we don't want to see what's there if it's different from what we wanted (remember how Veronica was so focused on getting married that she turned a blind eye to how much she was suffering in her relationship?). We don't want to feel the heartbreak and stress of letting go.

To avoid complicating your grief (and the other person's), it's important to pay attention to and honor the signs to move on.

My friend Patrick's story illustrates this. Patrick and his adult son had opened up their hearts and home to welcome his new wife and her 5-year-old child. Two years later, she wanted a divorce as her feelings for him had changed; he didn't see it coming. He struggled to make sense of the decision and come to terms with the fact that everything he'd believed about his marriage was now upended.

I talked with him about The Good Goodbye approach, and explained how powerful it can be to take control of moving through the letting-go process through intention and ritual. Patrick shared that he had Accepted his wife's decision to divorce. He was not denying what was facing him. He Understood where he was and where he wanted to be—he wanted to integrate the experience in a way that honored both the sacred union he and his wife shared, and the reality that they would be starting a new chapter with that union no longer in place. He was still working his way through the actions of Gratitude and Forgiveness, but he hoped that by engaging in a ritual, it would help him get there with more openness.

Although they hadn't finalized the divorce yet, Patrick adapted a six-step end-of-marriage ritual created by Rabbi Rachel Barenblat[49], and asked his wife to join him one evening to carry it out as a way of Saying Goodbye. With the permission of both Patrick and Rabbi Barenblat, I share details of their ritual here:

1. Opening Words

To establish the container for their Good Goodbye ritual and set their intentions, Patrick spoke the following words included in Rabbi Barenblat's ritual:

> *A marriage that has ended is like the first set of tablets and the covenant they represented. They were given in love, then they shattered. As we move into a new chapter of our lives, we carry hopes for new wholeness—and we also carry the broken pieces of our marriage, which are also holy.*
>
> *At our wedding we vowed to betroth ourselves to each other in righteousness, in loving kindness, and in compassion. May those same qualities be present as we disentangle our lives and separate from one another.*
>
> *As we open this ritual, we read the Surrender passage in "Ask an Angel."*

2. Prayer of Forgiveness

Patrick and his wife each took a turn asking for, and extending, forgiveness to the other person. They spoke

Rabbi Barenblat's "Prayer of Forgiveness" to each other to honor their shared desire for healing:

Eternal Friend, witness that I seek forgiveness:
for any injuries sustained over the course of our rela-
tionship whether by accident or willfully, carelessly or
purposely with words, deeds, thought, or attitudes now
or in previous incarnations.
May you not experience harm because of me.

Eternal Friend, witness that I forgive you
for any injuries sustained over the course of our rela-
tionship whether by accident or willfully, carelessly or
purposely with words, deeds, thought, or attitudes now
or in previous incarnations.
May you not experience harm because of me.

May the words of my mouth and the meditations of my
heart be acceptable to You.

3. New Beginning

In acknowledgment that they were starting a new chapter in which their union was dissolved, yet would continue to be connected as co-parents, Patrick and his wife both read the following passage written by Rabbi Barenblat:

Every ending is a new beginning. Although we will no longer be married in community, we will always be co-parents/stepparents to our children.

I promise to keep our children's needs at the forefront.

I promise never to speak ill of you to our children.

I promise to maintain good boundaries from separate households.

For the sake of our children, I promise to be as generous and flexible as life will permit.

I promise to join you in revisiting our arrangements as necessary, so that we can adapt our practices to meet the changing needs of our growing children.

I promise to do everything in my power to maintain a friendly relationship with you so that we can share in our children's joys and sorrows.

4. Expressing the Release

Patrick and his wife chose to honor their commitment to release each other and not try to control what happens in the future for each of them as they start separate lives. They sat in silence, and each wrote the following statement provided in Rabbi Barenblat's ritual on a piece of paper (filling in the blanks):

On the X day of the week, the Y day of the month of [Month] in the year [Year] from the creation of the world (equivalent to the secular date of [secular day, month, year]), here in [Place], I, [name], do willingly consent to release you, my wife/husband [English name].

We are no longer bound together. If you so choose, you may remarry freely. Your doorway is no longer my doorway. Wherever life takes you, may you go in peace.

5. The Cut

To symbolically mark and honor the cutting of their marriage union, Patrick and his wife spoke the following words as they tore up a copy of their marriage certificate:

As we tear into the heart of this document, divorce cuts deeply into our heart through divorcing. Our hearts have already been torn. May this ritual help us heal.

6. Closing

As discussed earlier, when you engage in a ritual, it's important to end it with closing words and actions to express appreciation for the ritual and all involved, and intentionally mark the ritual ceremony as complete.

Upon the closure of their ritual, Patrick and his wife spoke the following words which they adapted from Rabbi Barenblat's ritual:

> *At the end of our wedding we acknowledged those who were with us, and those who were not, a reminder that in every joyous occasion there is some sorrow. Now that our marriage has broken, may we find that even in this sorrowful occasion there is access to joy.*
>
> *Now go forth in peace, to life.*

By engaging in a beautiful Good Goodbye ritual, Patrick and his wife were able to memorialize their upcoming divorce in a way that allowed for Acceptance, Understanding, Gratitude, and Forgiveness. The ritual also was a symbolic moment of Saying Goodbye in which they could transform the love that brought them to marriage into a love that blessed each other as they went their separate ways.

How often do you stay in a friendship or relationship far longer than you want because you don't want to hurt the other person by ending the relationship? And when you finally do end it, do you part without so much as a "Thank you for our time together?" It's tempting to avoid the emotional pain that naturally comes with losing an attachment to someone you love, but as you've learned, avoidance does no one any good.

Call it out. Talk about it. Give yourself and the other person the chance to have a mature discussion about what's changed and how you'd both like to move forward. Trust that both of you can show up to share what is in your hearts. And if you know you're ready to move on and the other person isn't, you can, with compassion, let him or her know you need to close the chapter and Say Goodbye.

You can apply this to past relationships as well. If a relationship with someone went sour or just faded away with time, write a letter to that person to share what you celebrated about your time together and what you grieved having ended. Ask for forgiveness. Acknowledge your desire to rewrite a new story about why things ended—a story that integrates the good with the bad, the painful with the joyful.

You may also want to create your own Good Goodbye ritual for the past relationship that you can choose to do on your own, or invite the other person to do with you. Even if you don't get a response from the other person, you'll still be able to find closure on your end. Doing this in a way that's pure, intentional, and heartfelt will give you a new goodbye experience that empowers you to move forward with love.

Chapter XVII

The Final Goodbye

"I suppose in the end, the whole of life becomes an act of letting go, but what always hurts the most is not taking a moment to say goodbye."

-Yann Martel

One of the most powerful aspects of Saying Goodbye is intentionally recognizing a moment of completion, an ending. Endings give you a chance to reflect on your life and how you came to that point. And although reflecting about endings may be difficult and something you would rather avoid, there's a kind of goodbye everyone must face: the end of life.

The idea of Saying Goodbye to life—your own or someone else's—isn't something that is openly talked about. It doesn't come up at the dinner table or during happy hour. We're raised to fear death and not see the good in it. But if you've learned anything from this book, I hope it's that you get to choose what stories you hold on to and which ones you update or let go. The story you have around death can be one that frees you from the fear and allows you to surrender to it as a necessary part of life.

While I was writing this book, six people I knew died in the span of six months. Two of those deaths, the death of my grandmother and the death of a family friend, were ones where I was an active member in helping the families experience a Good Goodbye. The others included the death of a childhood friend; a former coworker; the unborn baby of a close friend; and the suicide of my twelve-year-old cousin. After the fourth death, I checked in with myself to see how I was doing with so many losses in such a short time. I wondered if I was unconsciously not coping with all the loss. After some reflection, I realized this was not the case. Years of living the philosophy of The Good Goodbye approach and coming to recognize that my own story of loss didn't have to set me back in life had given me the resilience to get through these losses with deeper Acceptance, Understanding, Gratitude, and Forgiveness.

During this time, I also was given the gift of an unplanned Good Goodbye. My 76-year-old father and I went out to lunch to spend some quality time together. Believe it or not, it was the first time we had spent time together, just the two of us. As we ate, I updated him on my book's progress. We talked about the past year and how the many losses I experienced gave me a chance to continue putting The Good Goodbye approach into practice. And finally, we talked about our relationship and my father's aging.

Growing up, my dad talked about death in a very matter-of-fact way. To him, death was just the next step after life; he believed that after death, there was life again in a new form. He would tell my mom, sister, and me that when he reached the age of 84, he would die. I remember feeling panic in my heart each time he'd say that. How did he know? What if I wasn't ready to let him go then? Could he live longer so we wouldn't have to face the end of his life?

That day at lunch, I asked my dad how he was doing. He replied that while his mind felt like he was in his 40s, his body reminded him daily that he wasn't. He talked about the increasing frustration he experienced as chronic pain limited his aging body. He had gotten to the point of Acceptance that he was nearing the end of his life. He explained that the reason he always talked so candidly to my sister and me about his aging process is because he didn't want us to be surprised by it when our turn came. He wanted us to feel ready for his departure, and also wanted us to be prepared for the last stage of our own lives. Also, given how my mom died suddenly without warning, my dad was giving my sister and me the opposite experience: he was going to prepare us for his last day on earth.

I asked him if he was still going to die at 84. With a calm conviction, he said, "Yes."

"What if you're still healthy then?" I asked.

"Well, I'd think about it and maybe keep going."

"And if you're not healthy? If your memory keeps fading?"

"No way. I don't want to be a burden to anyone. Then, I'm gone, mija. Bye-bye."

While talking to my dad about the one topic that I used to be so afraid to face, I realized that he was giving me the greatest gift ever. He was showing me how to have a Good Goodbye as his life came to an end. He was helping my sister and me Accept his aging and impending death. He shared his own process of Understanding how he felt being in the final stage of life and what he desired as an outcome. He wanted to feel positive about the remaining years of his life and live them in peace. He could hold Gratitude for the paradox of grief and celebration around death and create a story about it that empowered him. And he was teaching his daughters how to do the same in preparation for the day when he would no longer be with us. Whether he was aware of it or not, he was also giving my sister and me the chance to Forgive anything that remained unresolved in our relationship with him, if we needed to do so.

My dad was allowing us to Say Goodbye together. I listened to his desires, and committed to being part of making those desires a reality with him. We decided that together we would integrate the fear and grief of losing him with the celebration and joy of him still being here, as we embraced the love between us. We were thankful for the chance to be talking about this together and as we did, so much more Gratitude filled the space between us. Gratitude for all the lessons we learned, the hardships we overcame, the ways in which we healed past hurts through Forgiveness. How did we choose to ritualize this moment? With a clink of our water glasses and a prayer that we would never stop showing our love for one another, even after his body had stopped working.

You don't need to wait to create a Good Goodbye until a loss has happened. You can choose to experience it now while life continues.

Yes, it requires a lot of courage to face what you want to avoid because you're afraid of the pain it may cause. But if you avoid the situation, you'll miss out on the surprising magic that exists in boldly facing the fear and letting go with intention.

Death is the ultimate goodbye you'll face. Don't wait until the end to let your loved ones know what's in your heart. Start celebrating today and acknowledge what you'll grieve when life has passed. I can tell you firsthand that doing this now will give you and your loved ones the chance to feel a deep intimacy and bond, just as I felt with my dad during our lunch. You'll be filled with a peaceful strength and reminder of your resilience. You'll see that you do have the capacity to look goodbye straight in the eye and find greater compassion, grace, and healing, as you and your loved ones work together to plan for that final Good Goodbye.

Chapter XVIII

My Good Goodbye to You

"All the 'not readies,' all the 'I need time,' are understandable, but only for a short while. The truth is that there is never a 'completely ready,' there is never a really 'right time.'"

– Clarissa Pinkola Estés

Well, my friend, we've come to the end! I'm so honored you invested in reading this book and developed a new perspective on dealing with change—one that empowers you to approach things differently moving forward.

I hope you'll be able to apply The Good Goodbye approach to all kinds of change where you're losing an attachment to someone or something you value—whether it's a relationship, a job, a home, the death of a loved one or a pet, or outdated beliefs or stories. Use it to deal with the grief of a fresh loss as well as old wounds that need healing.

As a reminder, I've developed *The Good Goodbye Blueprint* which includes exercises, reflective prompts, and other suggested activities that will walk you through the actions of The Good Goodbye approach. The workbook is available for free download here:

https://drgladysato.com/the_good_goodbye_bonuses/

Customize the workbook as you see fit. Give yourself permission to start in any order. For example, if you feel ready to forgive, start with Forgiveness. Don't get caught up in whether you're doing things "right." Right is whatever feels best to you as you decide how to apply the approach in your life.

Learning how to embrace change and rewrite your goodbye story is not a solo journey. The more you can rally in the support of others, the more ease you'll find knowing that support is all around you. If you find that you've reached a point where you are stuck and don't feel you're able to get through things on your own, please reach out for help.

Professional therapists, counselors, pastors, healers, or other trusted sources of support can guide you and help you stay the course. Friends, family, and loved ones can listen, offer compassion, and give you reassurance that you'll find your way through. As you practice utilizing The Good Goodbye approach, you will deepen your level of emotional resilience, strengthen your self-soothing skills in times of stress, and become more aware of how you best can create the kind of goodbye that helps you thrive throughout the rest of your life.

Now, I'd love to ask for your help. Please consider sharing this book with someone who can use support to cope with change and loss differently. Maybe it's your friend who's going through a tough breakup. Or a colleague who was just laid off from a job. Perhaps your family member who hasn't let go of a past loss would benefit from a new way of letting go.

By sharing the book with others, you are helping change the way we approach change and goodbyes as a society. Together, we can empower ourselves to embrace goodbyes and use its magic to transform our lives.

To give the book as a gift, you can order a copy at: https://www.amazon.com/Good-Goodbye-Navigate-Change-Loss-ebook/dp/B074WCKHYB

If you are a leader of an organization that is going through a major organizational change and would like to purchase the book for your employees, please send an email to gladys@drgladysato.com for more information.

Story-sharing is a long-held practice of our ancestors; it gives you a chance to stand in your truth and pass on your knowledge to empower others who are fresh in their struggle. As you work through The Good Goodbye approach, I invite you to share your Good Goodbye story with others using #thegoodgoodbye hashtag on social media. Also, come join me and others in the members-only site at:

https://drgladysato.com/the_good_goodbye_bonuses/

This site gives you access to an amazing community of change makers who lift each other up with their inspiring stories of change, support each other, and serve as reminders that you're never alone. I'm in this space regularly to reinforce the application of The Good Goodbye approach, answer questions as they come up, and shepherd everyone involved to step into a new chapter more confident, open, and eager for what unfolds.

If you aren't interested in accessing the members-only site, you can also send me your Good Goodbye story via email to: gladys@drgladysato.com. I would be honored to read about your experience, and with your permission, I may share your story on my website to encourage others to create their own Good Goodbye experience.

You've got this one life.

Make it amazing.

Put the criticism, self-doubt, or worry on pause.

Dare yourself to step out of your comfort zone.

Take that leap.

Then watch the magic unfold.

Goodbye to you, my friend. Thank you for joining me on this journey.

Con gratitud,

Dr. Gladys Ato

Acknowledgments

"As we express our gratitude, we must never forget that the highest appreciation is not to utter words, but to live by them."

-John F. Kennedy

There are a myriad of influences that help shape a new creation and bring it to birth. It's no different when writing a book. I especially want to thank the following people who were instrumental in helping me write and publish *The Good Goodbye*. They believed in my message and made it their mission to champion me to excel.

Maria Ato, on November 7, 2003, you showed me what it meant to experience a Good Goodbye. You planted the seed in my heart and 14 years later, that seed has grown into a beautiful creation. You are the reason for this book, Mommy. Through your spirit, you have guided me, showered me with love, and brought the most amazing angels to my life at just the right time to make this book a reality. May this book be a testament to the incredible life you had and the hundreds of hearts you touched through your love. And through your death, I thank you for giving me a new life. I will always make the most of it to honor you. I love you, Mommy and miss you Every.Single.Day.

To my father, Luis Ato, you always told Jackie and me, "You are who you are because you choose to be that way." Thank you for seeing in me what I failed to see for so many years and believing in my ability to keep growing into my best self. I am so grateful for the sacrifices you and Mommy made to give us a life better than your own. You've been there with me to say goodbye to the layers of hardship that our family has endured over the years, and you did it for one reason: Love. I love you, Papi and will always cherish the ways each of us invested in making our relationship the strongest it could be.

Jackie Ato-Patterson—my little one—you are the best sister a person could ever have. You've been there every step of the way as my cheerleader, confidant, friend, and reality checker when I believed I couldn't make this book happen. More than anything, you've been with me on this path of healing from Mommy's death and have become an incredible woman. I'm so proud of you. Thank you for reading every version of the book, catching last minute edits, and doing everything you can to make me feel like the luckiest sister on earth to have you by my side. I love you, little one.

Dr. Irene McLoughlin, for 8 years, you held me in the safe space of therapy as I figured out how to say goodbye to my mom and build my life as a young, motherless woman. You helped me unlock the door to my heart where healing and self-love awaited. Thank you for giving me the courage to create a legacy that would make my mom proud and showing me how to create Good Goodbyes each time a relationship ended.

Amit West, you have been my healer, intuitive guide, connector to my mother, and friend. You guided me in times when I didn't know how to create my own Good Goodbyes and showed me how to infuse my actions with spiritual magic. You gave me the courage to answer the question, "What does Gladys have to say about goodbyes," and helped me spread my wings even more than I thought possible. I love you, Anxo Terra and honor your sacredness.

Thank you, Dr. Gary Burkholder, for being my pillar of support through the most challenging professional experiences I've had. Your steadfast wisdom and gentle guidance kept me going when I wanted to quit. You never stop short of helping me achieve excellence. Thank you for everything you did to support me in writing this book and making my dreams come true.

Lizzie Stevenson, Kristin Reinsberg, and Dr. Maryam Hafezi, you each helped me learn how to *wonder* about the ways we form our attachments in life. In the times when I found myself having less and less time to wonder, you stayed with me, gently offering your support. And when I regained my wonderment, you joined me to think through all the ways that I could share the importance of my message with others. I am so blessed to have you as my great friends and brilliantly talented colleagues.

Jimmy Tilley (aka: Miz Eva Sensitiva), Dr. Angel Nguyen, Majal Logan, Crystal Martinez, Dr. Renato Almanzor, Sandra Moulton, and Stephanie Peterson, I'm deeply honored for the pivotal roles you had in making this book come alive. Thank you for showing me how multi-layered a Good Goodbye experience can be and helping me think about the approach through a new lens. You are each a testament to the beauty that's found when one learns to let go with grace.

From the first moment we talked about the book, Carey Jones, you listened with a careful ear and a gentle heart to my vision. Through your editing genius, you helped bring that vision out in the best way possible. I'm deeply grateful that you went above and beyond what was expected to transform this book from an emotional outpouring of nonsensical thoughts to a comprehensive, engaging journey of change and loss.

Thank you, Stef Etow, for giving my book her beautiful skin. The deep care and thought you put into designing a spectacular book cover, graphics, and strategies to share my book's message fills my heart with so much gratitude and joy. I'm blessed to have experienced your constant love and attention to ensure this book would be received with open arms and hearts.

Julia Wells, Sarah Barbour, and Heidi Sutherlin, you have each been pivotal in me sharing this book with celebration and joy! Julia, thank you for your perfectly timed reminders to give "zero fucks" when I was flooded in doubt and helping me create an awesome book launch strategy. Sarah, I thank you for your compassion, strategic mind, and grace as a book coach to help me stay focused and get this book in as many hands as possible. Heidi, your enthusiasm for completing the important last step of formatting my book infused me with excitement at just the right time. I'm so grateful to each of you for giving me confidence when I most needed it.

Thank you God-Spirit-Universe for infusing me with the words that fill this book. Thank you for surrounding me with the blessings of angels who have shown up as friends, family members, lovers, teachers, colleagues, strangers, and pets to guide me on my journey. I am grateful for the ways you've shown me to always find the good in life and never stop growing. May this book be the end of several chapters of heartbreak that my family lineage has endured, and the start of a new legacy that will empower the hearts of all those who walk after me on this path of truth.

Con gratitud.

Meet the Author

Dr. Gladys Ato champions individuals and organizations to evolve through change in order to reach their highest potential. She is a change leadership and personal growth expert, psychologist, speaker, and author of the book, *The Good Goodbye: How to Navigate Change and Loss in Life, Love, and Work.*

Recognized as a Latina leader by Hispanic Executive magazine and a Women Worth Watching in Education winner by Profiles in Diversity Journal, Dr. Ato has been featured in NPR, Thrive Global, Elephant Journal, Harness Magazine, and other publications. She established her business and blog, Bridging Consciousness, in 2016 and in less than a year, her blog was named one of the top 50 consciousness websites in the world.

Prior to founding Bridging Consciousness, Dr. Ato had a successful career as a top performing C- suite executive leader, psychotherapist, university educator, and consultant. She was the CEO/president and provost of The National Hispanic University and vice president of academic affairs, undergraduate studies department chair, and assistant faculty at Argosy University, San Francisco

Bay Area. She developed a strong reputation for successfully leading teams and organizations through various changes in the organizational life cycle.

Dr. Ato has mentored and guided exceptional leaders, talented entrepreneurs, dedicated teachers, consultants, and rising stars to excel in achieving their full potential. She has served hundreds of individuals and several organizations as a psychotherapist, consultant, board president and vice president, and supervisor in various medical, mental health, education, and nonprofit settings.

Today, Dr. Ato works with clients through private leadership mentoring, online personal development courses, and speaking engagements. You can find her strolling the streets of San Francisco with her pup, Lovebug, hunting for estate sale treasures, nourishing her passion for style, and satisfying her foodie palate.

Meet Dr. Ato, and receive free resources on leadership and personal development, at drgladysato.com.

Cited Works

Part 1

1. Plummer, K. (2001). The call of life stories in ethno-
    graphic research. In P. Atkinson, A. Coffey, S.
    Delamont, J. Loftland, & L. Loftland (Eds.), *Handbook
    of ethnography* (pp. 395- 406). Thousand Oaks, CA:
    Sage.

2. Ainsworth, M. (1973). The development of infant-
    mother attachment. In B. Caldwell & HN Ricciuti
    (Eds.), *Review of child development research* (pp. 1–
    94). Chicago, IL: University of Chicago Press.

3. Bowlby, J. (1969). Attachment and loss, Vol. 1: At-
    tachment. *Attachment and loss.* New York, NY: Basic
    Books.

4. Folkman, S. (2011). *The Oxford handbook of stress,
    health, and coping.* New York, NY: Oxford University
    Press.

5. Perry, B. D., & Pollard, R. (1998). Homeostasis, stress, trauma, and adaptation: A neurodevelopmental view of childhood trauma. *Child and Adolescent Psychiatric Clinics of North America, 7*(1), 33-51.

6. Bridges, L. J., & Grolnick, W. S. (1995). The development of emotional self-regulation in infancy and early childhood. In N. Eisenberg (Ed.), *Social development, Vol. 15. Review of personality and social psychology* (pp. 185-211). Thousand Oaks, CA: Sage.

7. van der Kolk, B. A., & Fisler, R. E. (1994). Childhood abuse and neglect and loss of self-regulation. *Bulletin of the Menninger Clinic, 58*(2), 145-168.

8. van der Kolk, B. A. (1996). The complexity of adaptation to trauma: Self-regulation, stimulus discrimination, and characterological development. In B. A. van der Kolk, A. C. McFarlane, & L. Weisaeth (Eds.), *Traumatic stress: The effects of overwhelming experience on mind, body, and society* (pp. 182-213). New York, NY: Guilford Press.

9. Rutter, M. (1985). Resilience in the face of adversity. Protective factors and resistance to psychiatric disorder. *The British Journal of Psychiatry, 147*(6), 598-611.

10. Beasley, M., Thompson, T., & Davidson, J. (2003). Resilience in response to life stress: The effects of coping style and cognitive hardiness. *Personality and Individual Differences, 34*(1), 77-95.

11. Kumar, S. M. (2005). *Grieving mindfully: A compassionate and spiritual guide to coping with loss.* Oakland, CA: New Harbinger Publications.

12. Kubler-Ross, E. (1969). *On death and dying.* New York, NY: Macmillan.

13. Mikulincer, M., & Shaver, P. R. (2007). *Attachment in adulthood: Structure, dynamics, and change.* New York, NY: Guilford Press.

14. Selye, H. (1950). *Stress: The physiology and pathology of exposure to stress.* Montreal: Acta Medica Publication.

15. Lazarus, R. S. (1993). From psychological stress to the emotions: A history of changing outlooks. *Annual Review of Psychology, 44*(1), 1-22.

16. Tallon, A. (1997). *Head and heart: Affection, cognition, volition as triune consciousness.* New York, NY: Fordham University Press.

17. McCraty, R., Atkinson, M., Tomasino, D., & Bradley, R. T. (2009). The coherent heart Heart-brain interactions, psychophysiological coherence, and the emergence of system-wide order. *Integral Review: A Transdisciplinary & Transcultural Journal for New Thought, Research, & Praxis, 5*(2), 10-115.

18. McCraty, R. (2003). *Heart-brain neurodynamics. The making of emotions.* Boulder Creek, CA: Heart Math Research Center, Institute of Heart Math, Publication No. 03-015.

19. Shear, K., & Shair, H. (2005). Attachment, loss, and complicated grief. *Developmental Psychobiology, 47*(3), 253-267.

Part 2

20. Hayes, S. C., Strosahl, K. D., & Wilson, K. G. (2011). *Acceptance and commitment therapy: The process and practice of mindful change.* New York, NY: Guilford Press.

21. Das, L. S. (2009). *Awakening the Buddha within: Eight steps to enlightenment.* New York, NY: Broadway Books.

22. Nowinski, J., & Baker, S. (1992). *The twelve-step facilitation handbook: A systematic approach to early recovery from alcoholism and addiction.* San Francisco, CA: Jossey-Bass.

23. Snyder, M., & Uranowitz, S. W. (1978). Reconstructing the past: Some cognitive consequences of person perception. *Journal of Personality and Social Psychology, 36*(9), 941-950.

24. McCraty, R., Atkinson, M., & Tomasino, D. (2001). *Science of the heart: exploring the role of the heart in human performance.* Boulder Creek, CA: HeartMath Research Center, Institute of HeartMath, Publication No. 01–001.

25. Mezirow, J. (1990). How critical reflection triggers transformative learning. *Fostering critical reflection in adulthood* (pp. 1-20). San Francisco, CA: Jossey Bass.

26. Schacter, D. L., Addis, D. R., & Buckner, R. L. (2007). Remembering the past to imagine the future: The prospective brain. *Nature Reviews Neuroscience, 8*(9), 657-661.

27. Gilovich, T. (1981). Seeing the past in the present: The effect of associations to familiar events on judgments and decisions. *Journal of Personality and Social Psychology, 40*(5), 797-808.

28. Watkins, P. C., Van Gelder, M., & Frias, A. (2011). Furthering the science of gratitude. In S.J. Lopez & C.R. Snyder (Eds.), *Oxford handbook of positive psychology* (pp. 437-445). Oxford: Oxford University Press.

29. Wood, A. M., Joseph, S., & Linley, P. A. (2007). Coping style as a psychological resource of grateful people. *Journal of Social and Clinical Psychology, 26*(9), 1076-1093.

30. Toussaint, L., & Webb, J. R. (2005). Theoretical and empirical connections between forgiveness, mental

health and well-being. In E.L. Worthington (Ed.), *Handbook of forgiveness* (pp. 349-362). New York, NY: Routledge.

31. Kuhl, J., Quirin, M., & Koole, S. L. (2015). Being someone: The integrated self as a neuropsychological system. *Social and Personality Psychology Compass, 9*(3), 115-132.

32. Maslow, A. (1962). Some basic propositions of a growth and self-actualization psychology. In A. Combs (Ed.), *Perceiving, behaving, becoming: A new focus for education, Association for Supervision and Curriculum Development 1962 yearbook* (pp. 34-39). Washington, DC: Association for Supervision and Curriculum Development.

33. Danesh, H. B. (2000). *Psychology of spirituality: From divided self to integrated self*. New Delhi: Sterling Publishers Pvt. Ltd.

34. Deci, E. L., & Ryan, R. M. (1990). A motivational approach to self: Integration in personality. In R. Dienstbier (Ed.), *Nebraska symposium on motivation: Vol. 38. Perspectives on motivation* (pp. 237-288). Lincoln, NE: University of Nebraska Press.

35. Tart, C. T. (2010). Toward an evidence-based spirituality: Some glimpses of an evolving vision. *Subtle Energies & Energy Medicine Journal Archives, 21*(1), 7-38.

36. Ingersoll, R. E. (2007). Spirituality and counseling: The dance of magic and effort. In O. Morgan (Ed.), *Counseling and spirituality: Views from the profession* (pp. 230-247). New York, NY: Lakasha Press.

37. Graf, F. (1997). *Magic in the ancient world* (F. Philip Trans.). Cambridge, MA: Harvard University Press.

38. Combs, A., & Holland, M. (2001). *Synchronicity: Through the eyes of science, myth, and the trickster.* Boston, MA: Da Capo Press.

39. Vyse, S. A. (2013). *Believing in magic: The psychology of superstition-Updated edition.* New York, NY: Oxford University Press.

40. Longo, D. A., & Peterson, S. M. (2002). The role of spirituality in psychosocial rehabilitation. *Psychiatric Rehabilitation Journal, 25*(4), 333-340.

41. Ivtzan, I., Chan, C. P., Gardner, H. E., & Prashar, K. (2013). Linking religion and spirituality with psychological well-being: Examining self-actualisation, meaning in life, and personal growth initiative. *Journal of Religion and Health, 52*(3), 915-929.

42. Cloninger, C. R. (2006). The science of well-being: An integrated approach to mental health and its disorders. *World Psychiatry, 5*(2), 71-76.

43. Hemmingson, M. (2009). Anthropology of the memorial: Observations and reflections on American cultural rituals associated with death. *Forum Qualitative Sozialforschung/Forum: Qualitative Social Research, 10*(3), Art. 6.

44. Williams, M. (1997). Helping people to say goodbye. *British Medical Journal, 315*(7103), 317-318.

45. Magolda, P. M. (2003). Saying goodbye: An anthropological examination of a commencement ritual. *Journal of College Student Development, 44*(6), 779-796.

46. Carrico, K. (2012). Ritual. *Cultural Anthropology.* Retrieved from https://culanth.org/curated_collections/4-ritual.

47. Somé, M. P. (1997). *Ritual: Power, healing and community*. New York, NY: Penguin Books.

48. Imber-Black, E. (1991). Rituals and the healing process. In F. Walsh & M. McGoldrick (Eds.), *Living beyond loss: Death in the family* (pp. 207- 223). New York, NY: Norton.

Part 3

49. Barenblat, R. (2016, September 18). *A ritual for ending a marriage*. Retrieved from http://velveteenrabbi.blogs.com/blog/2016/09/a-ritual-for-ending-a-marriage.html.

Made in the USA
San Bernardino, CA
18 October 2017